*Alcott's*

# IMAGINARY HEROES

*The* **LITTLE WOMEN** *Legacy*

*Edited by*

**MERRY GORDON**

**MARNAE KELLEY**

**PINK UMBRELLA BOOKS**

Published by Pink Umbrella Books
www.pinkumbrellapublishing.com
Gordon, Merry, Ed.
Kelley, Marnae, Ed.

Alcott's imaginary heroes: The Little Women legacy/
Merry Gordon, Marnae Kelley.

ISBN: 9780998516288

Library of Congress Control Number: 2018951270

*For Louisa—*
*and the generations of little women*
*who grew up with her*

# Contents

# Introduction: Rediscovering *Little Women*

*"I don't know whether the study of Shakespeare helped her to read character, or the natural instinct of a woman for what was honest, brave, and strong, but while endowing her imaginary heroes with every perfection under the sun, Jo was discovering a live hero, who interested her in spite of many human imperfections."*

—"A Friend," *Little Women*

Louisa May Alcott saved my life (or at least my motherhood and marriage).

It was 2004, and I had just given birth to my first child—not "the deepest and tenderest" experience of my life, as *Little Women* had assured me it would be. It was brutal. My body felt foreign, no longer my own. Everything ached. Endless failed attempts at nursing proved demoralizing and exhausting. I lashed out at my bewildered husband and regarded my newborn with guilty indifference. Deep into the night I sobbed as I sat half-dressed in an oversized t-shirt and prayed for my milk to come in, or for a swift and relatively painless death. (Either one would have been fine by that point.)

Between pumping and feeding, I didn't sleep—so I read. A stack of my favorite dog-eared books from childhood sat beside me, comfort reads for relentless nights. *The Chronicles of Narnia. Anne of Green Gables.*

And one evening, just before collapse set in, I picked up *Little Women.*

I thought I remembered it. I'd read it a thousand times. Meg, Jo and Amy were childhood heroines, archetypes of feminine virtue. Beth was such a saint Alcott had no choice but to kill the girl off. And Marmee—Marmee was all wifely perfection and motherly benevolence and everything I wasn't.

Marmee was why I didn't want to open the book.

Sure enough, I thumbed through the pages and there she was, dispensing advice like some Civil War era fortune cookie oracle of womanhood:

"When you feel discontented, think over your blessings, and be grateful."

"Don't cry so bitterly, but remember this day, and resolve with all your soul that you will never know another like it."

"Watch and pray, dear, never get tired of trying, and never think it is impossible to conquer your fault."

I wanted to throw the book across the room. College lit classes had taught me cynicism, and I knew outdated, sexist, sentimental tripe when I saw it.

Or so I thought.

Marmee's maxims, saccharine though they seemed, struck a chord of truth that night. I kept reading. The story had never resonated like this. I noticed things I hadn't before. Marmee got angry. Beth was painfully timid, almost pathologically so. Meg was vain, and Amy, selfish. Jo—dear, sweet, irrepressible Jo—was reckless, often self-sabotaging. And all of them struggled against self and against type. They were not the characters I thought they were.

I understood then that Louisa May Alcott had seen with prescient eyes into the conflicted womanhood that was my everyday life: in the lives of the March women is the battle between storm and calm, vanity and sacrifice, ambition and duty, career and family, passion and congruity.

I learned to see the sisters with fresh eyes, to appreciate them for their strengths *and* weaknesses. I learned to appreciate my own weaknesses and conquer them if I could.

More importantly, I learned what Jo learned, that sometimes it's best to shelve our imaginary heroes in favor of what is "honest, brave, and strong"—and ultimately, imperfect.

By the time I finished *Little Women*, mother, child and marriage were all intact. I could be a marmee and learn from Marmee without *being* Marmee (or the imaginary hero I had thought her to be).

ꕤ

In this, the 150th anniversary year of the novel's publication, we invite you to celebrate Alcott's *Little Women*.

In our essays we celebrate the novel's messages—the contradictory as well as the comforting. We celebrate what might have been and what is. We celebrate Beth's dolls, Meg's dresses, Amy's clothespinned nose, and Jo's precious manuscript. We take *Little Women* with us across the world, into New York City tenements teeming with immigrants, into the slums of Mumbai, to church and to work. We take it socially and globally. Most of all, despite its "many human imperfections," we take it personally.

We celebrate our imaginary heroes and the power of Alcott's pen, still relevant after all these years.

—Merry Gordon, Phoenix, July 2018

# Literary Lessons

*by Marlowe Daly*

ഗ

"But you guys, I *promise* you will love it. You *have* to keep reading," Char implores the class.

She is noticeably distressed that not all of the students in our class are in love with *Little Women* after reading the first eight chapters. Her shoulders roll forward and then back as she turns her head. She's always been engaged in discussions, but *Little Women* seems to have awoken a deeper, stronger passion than I have seen in her before. Looking at her fills me with anticipation.

My eyes scan the group. We have arranged the tables into a large, slightly lopsided rectangle, with one end of a table sticking out like a chimney. Fifteen of the seventeen faces peer at me, as if waiting for me to validate Char's promise. Two of the students look down at their journals, afraid that I will demand their "second impressions." These two alone seem to not have done the reading. The class has already shared first reactions, and it's clear that their feelings are vast and wide on this one. Some, like Char, read *Little Women* as children and loved it.

"It's the reason I love literature!" Char later confided.

Others, like me, read it as children but didn't love it then. Now that they are English majors (or feminists, or adults), they find it more interesting. Some are reading it for the first time and not sure what to think about it. Some are feeling bored or unconnected. Laura, an only child, wonders if maybe she just can't 'get it' because she doesn't have any sisters. Henry, the lone male student in this group, says he never had much interest in reading *Little Women*, but now that he's started, he is intrigued.

Later on, another student will single him out, reminding her peers, "But Henry likes it!" Henry is always quiet and gracious when called out like this, usually offering a charming and slightly mischievous smile. He claims he doesn't relate to Laurie Laurence "at *all*," and yet he is comfortable and happy among this group of women. When we discuss the "Castles in the Air" chapter, Henry sees it as a call to Thoreau and Transcendentalism. I feel happy to be able to share with them that Thoreau was one of Alcott's mentors, and that he led the Alcott girls around the woods of Concord teaching them lessons in botany.

This is a good class. I've gotten so spoiled lately that I forget what it feels like to have a bad class. My heart fills with appreciation for these students. It sits so heavy in my chest that I actually feel it as a pain. They are special. When we interview potential faculty, I can speak honestly about the pleasures of teaching our students. Of course, there are also the heartbreaks. They have jobs and relationships and family commitments. They get Pell grants and rent their textbooks. Their parents often did not go to college. Some of them are veterans. A few are grandparents. Some of them have never been outside the Northwest. A few have never been to Seattle.

They tease me because I don't know when hunting season starts. Or ends.

They are smart. They are usually white and Christian. If they fall asleep in class, it's not because they've been out partying, but it may be that they worked a graveyard shift or had to take care of siblings late into the night. Sometimes there is domestic violence in their homes. I have called security because I worried a student was in danger, and I have directed students to community resources so they can avoid mid-semester homelessness.

Some of these students write beautifully. Others offer raw, original interpretations of literature but struggle to construct an academic paragraph.

I don't necessarily expect them to like *Little Women,* but I am gratified that they do. When I show them scenes from the different films, I love that they giggle at Katherine Hepburn's antics and cry along with Winona Ryder when Beth dies. They disapprove of Liz Taylor being *older* than Margaret O'Brien, because they know, of course, that Amy March is the youngest sister.

I am meeting with a student from a different class in the campus coffee shop. After she leaves, I look up and see Char and Emily and Annie sitting at a table together.

"Hi! Can we talk to you?" Char asks.

I make my way across the café. Annie is wiping her eyes.

"It's just sad," she says. Ah. I can see that she knows that Beth is going to die. They have their copies of *Little Women* out on the table and have been reading together. For some reason, this seems unbelievably sweet to me.

"Do you girls want to try a free drink?" the barista yells across the room. "I have enough for three." I am not included in the invitation, but it makes me happy to see my students get free drinks. Emily goes to the counter and brings back three cups. Whatever the free drink is, it's not coffee. It is pink with tiny squares of ice in it. They drink them down quickly and observe that Beth's death is sad, but not because they sympathize with her. Instead, they sympathize with Jo, who is devastated by it. I think they are probably on to something.

"I always liked the character of Beth, though," Emily confesses. She points out that Alcott begins foreshadowing Beth's death in Chapter Four.

"It was always coming."

The pink drink seems to revive them and they wax merrily on their attachment to *Little Women.*

"I'd never read it before, and now I'm obsessed with it!" Annie admits. They all laugh.

"My boyfriend says I like this book better than him," she adds.

Now I laugh. We chat some more about Alcott and the book and being an English major and a professor. As Annie's boyfriend arrives, I make my exit. They do not know it, but they've made my heart hurt again. This little conversation reminds me of why I live in this small town without a Trader Joe's or a *tortillería* or an Asian market.

This was not the place I imagined myself, but it is the place I live and work. It is the place I get to teach literature to these lovely people. And in spite of being an Alcott scholar, this is the first time I have attempted to teach *Little Women* here. I've been here six years. I've taught *Hospital Sketches* and "My Contraband" several times, but never *Little Women.*

*Why not Little Women?* Why did I wait so long, when it seems like such a natural teaching choice for a professor like me? I guess the novel is too long. It requires a full three weeks of the semester. But am I really going to use that rationale when I regularly teach *Moby-Dick* and *Uncle Tom's Cabin*? I guess it is because I am still conflicted about *Little Women*.

Is it a feminist novel?

Is it an empowering novel?

Is it *good?*

To all of these questions I might answer yes, … and no. *Little Women* empowers girls and women by telling their stories and by insisting that their stories are important. Yet some of its more overt messages to girls—that they should suppress their anger in order to be womanly or that they should not write anything sensational or improper—are not the messages I want young women to internalize. Really, if I am honest, I find these messages deeply troubling.

But, of course, it's a good novel. It wouldn't have lasted 150 years in the public consciousness if it weren't. It couldn't have inspired so many films and adaptations if it weren't. Yet as a professor of literature, I've learned that it's hard to pin down what makes a good novel. In class, we talk about how a novel affects us, whether we can relate to character choices, and whether the language is original or beautiful.

In *Little Women,* Alcott undoubtedly creates interesting characters. Meg, Jo, Beth, and Amy feel as real to me now as they did when I first encountered them at the age of ten. And even if ten-year-old me didn't like the March girls quite as much as Trixie Belden or Anne Shirley, they still became part of the repertoire of female characters I embodied in my imaginary play and juvenile writing.

But *Little Women* is imperfect. It was written hastily. It is episodic. It can be preachy.

Is it ambiguous? Yes!

Maybe the real reason I haven't taught *Little Women* is because I am afraid. *What if students hate it? Even worse: what if they don't learn?* Later, when I read their reading response journals, I will see their changing reactions to the novel. I will see that most of the students who started off unsure about whether the novel was going to work for them ended up liking it. Emily will even ask her mom to re-read the novel so that they can talk about it together over spring break.

As I walk home, I replay the coffee shop conversation in my mind. It was pretty wonderful. I know I am grinning and maybe even talking to myself a little bit as I stroll through campus and my neighborhood. I catch myself doing this more and more often and know that I am well on my way to being a caricature of a batty professor, walking into trees while reciting poetry with her glasses all askew.

"Christopher Columbus!", Jo would say. I was silly to be afraid. They are loving *Little Women* because of its ambiguity and because of its problems. They are divided about whether Laurie and Amy will be happy together and confused about whether Laurie and Jo ever *could* be happy together. They care about the biographical parallels and they're interested in the novel's discussion of class and privilege. These tiny moments over pink drinks with students reaffirm for me that teaching matters. Reading matters. What I do matters. As I walk home thinking about this, I trip on a branch and nearly fall.

Clumsily, I straighten myself up, look around, and keep walking. This is who I've become.

I am a small-town professor who teaches *Little Women.*

## About the Author

***Marlowe Daly*** teaches American literature, writing, and interdisciplinary humanities classes at Lewis-Clark State College. She lives with her family in Idaho, where she devotes large amounts of her time to walking along the Snake River with her dog. She has spent years thinking about Louisa May Alcott's fascination with the problems of being a professional woman writer in the nineteenth century. Marlowe's work has been published in *ESQ, Pedagogy in American Literary Studies, The Blue Hour, Northern Cardinal Review,* and *Bone Parade.*

# A Lesson in Love: The Importance of Beth March

*by Caitlin Horne*

∽

Beth March is not my favorite March sister. Of course she isn't.

My unwavering favorite is, has always been, and will always be Jo—and there's probably nothing I can say about how deep my love for Jo March runs that hasn't already been said hundreds of thousands of times. Jo March is the pinnacle of what makes a character timeless: she's a figure that almost everyone can relate to in a small way, and that a good percentage can relate to in a huge way. She's the heart of Louisa May Alcott poured onto a page, and, generation by generation, people like me have been picking up Alcott's masterpiece and feeling this heart overflowing, filling out corners of our own characters, and keeping the author's flame burning after a hundred and fifty years.

This isn't to claim that Jo March is exclusively the best-loved *Little Women* character, because different people find glimpses of themselves in different places. Jo is so easy to relate to, though; I felt, discovering her, that I'd rarely before felt so close to a character, and numberless other readers have had the same experience. There is a lot of love and recognition for Jo to be found in the world.

All of this begs one giant question: do we give *Beth* the love and recognition she deserves?

During my most recent re-read of *Little Women*, at a time when my Jo-like ambition was at an all-time high, I was surprised to find that it was actually Beth who kept catching my attention. It's widely acknowledged that the sisterly love between Jo and Beth in *Little Women* is one of the deepest and most important relationships in any of Alcott's novels; it is clear that the love between Louisa and her real sister Elizabeth translated into her work in a pure and beautiful way. The sisters have such perfectly complementary characters that when they are put together they understand both their shared loves and their differences in a way that can only enrich both of their lives.

Perhaps I'm wrong, but I've always found it telling how of all the sisters, it is Beth whose name is not altered from her real-life counterpart. It is Beth—in the book, and perhaps in reality too—who really shapes the tale of *Little Women*, and, most importantly for me, the character of Jo March.

Beth is Jo's morality. She is a reminder of all that Jo finds most precious and most unreachable in the world: humility, patience, quiet dedication. The process of loving and losing her sister changed Louisa and changed Jo, leading Jo to realize that while she was out searching for "something splendid" to do with her life, her sister was already doing splendid things—even if no one quite understood it until she was gone. For Beth, "something splendid" was not grand or ambitious, but a lifetime spent giving out kindness and simple love. For me, that has always been the heart of *Little Women*: Jo's discovery that the greatest courage sometimes manifests itself in the quietest ways. In the end, Jo's fate is not fame or riches, but a humbler life that she spends sharing love with others. Would she ever have done this without Beth's influence, both during her life and her death?

Beth is, as Alcott states, not "an angel, but a very human little girl." She *is* flawed. Her character deserves love for demonstrating a beautiful human soul, with her sweet nature, love of music, kindness and simple dreams. Despite this, while there are undoubtedly readers out there who identify with Beth's struggles, her role in the story has often seemed more to me like a moral message, an embodiment of goodness and kindness, than a character. There is something so inherently sweet and rosy about Beth that just makes her seem a little out of reach.

It was only during my most recent re-read that this almost unrealistically sweet characterization suddenly made sense to me. *Little Women* is an exploration of four beautiful sisters, but most of all it's an exploration of Jo, an examination of family life from the perspective of the wild, storm-in-a-teacup, loving-but-flawed Jo March.

In this context, how could Beth be anything *other* than the morality of the novel? Beth has such a quiet, ever-present influence on her sister that her role was never to develop into an relatable, lively character, but to become a role model in her own sweet way, just as she was a role model for Jo.

This isn't to diminish Beth into nothing more than a lesson for Jo—she is, after all, a wonderful character anyway—but when considering the sisters, I realized that Beth's presence in the novel is much like her presence in the family dynamic: as readers, we don't see quite how important she is until we try to imagine *Little Women* without her.

Because here is the crux of the matter: while the majority of readers might identify most deeply with Jo's journey—or Amy's, or Meg's, or Marmee's—who is it that shapes these journeys the most?

It is Beth.

Subtly, sweetly, unassumingly, Beth worms her way into her family's and friends' hearts and into ours, just as the real Elizabeth inspired in Louisa a deep and profound love. Beth demonstrates that there are many ways to be kind and brave, both through her own struggles, and by inspiring her sisters to value kindness and bravery, and act on these values in their own unique ways.

It is always fantastic when a novel features characters that are kind, warm, and gentle, despite their struggles, despite their wants, despite their longings, despite their imperfections. It is even better when readers experience the importance of these people through the eyes of those who feel the influence the deepest.

Jo March is almost universally loved, but Jo March wouldn't be Jo March without the influence of her quietest sister … and in fact, the same can be said for almost every character in the novel.

Beth is the morality of the novel, yes—but she is also its heart.

---

## About the Author

---

***Caitlin Horne*** lives in the English countryside, where, like her hero Jo March, she spends most of her time crying over novels, scribbling in notebooks, cutting off her hair for charity, and dreaming of doing "something very splendid." She first discovered *Little Women* at twelve years old while helping to clear out her grandparents' attic, in the process of which her grandma's own childhood copy of the book was unearthed. Soon after, she managed to persuade her school book club to read the novel together, an endeavor which ended with them dressing up for World Book Day as the March family, wearing costumes borrowed from the town theatre, or else fashioned from charity shop fabric and a mother's innovative use of curtain wire. Her copy of the novel—now bound together with copious amounts of tape—remains one of her most precious possessions, along with the lessons she learned from it.

# Globetrotting with Amy: Why She Deserves Her Happy Ending

*by Nomisha C. Kurian*

ഗ

Vevay. For normal people, the name denotes a scenic Swiss town; for excitable Alcott fans, Vevay is home to possibly the most polarizing scene in *Little Women*. Alcott sketches Laurie and Amy's love as gently and rosily as she does Vevay's hills and winds. Yet for many, the romance staggers under the weight of the elephant lumbering around the (château) room: why *Amy*?

Scruffy, defiant, and eternally endearing, Jo inspires the kind of love and devotion in readers that only classic underdogs can. As Laurie's visions of golden hair and blue ribbons erase Jo from his romantic horizons, crowds of defensive fans picket in her wake. Comments like "I can't believe who he ended up with!" "How could you pick insipid Amy over Jo, who has a thousand times more character?" "UGH, Amy," proliferate on *Little Women* blogs. Perhaps such reader resentment stems from the vivid contrast between the two most antagonistic March sisters. If Jo, championing a clear set of principles and values, is a sturdy full stop, then Amy, brimming with moral ambiguity, is a bit of a question mark. Characters who seem to get everything they want—as sunnily as Vevay's cloudless blue skies—are never easy to love.

Yet, as an adult, I have begun to savor Amy's happiness in Vevay. Throughout university, I've crammed my life into suitcases and travel diaries. I study at Cambridge, but my family is based in Mumbai and Singapore. Living in three different countries simultaneously has made me appreciate the richness and complexity of identity. My Netflix queue features BBC and Bollywood; my wardrobe houses somber grey coats and bright red saris; my takeaway boxes hold crispy fish and chips and hot biryani. As I laugh over the contrasts and embrace the dizzying magic of change, I do what I think all bookworms do: look to my favorite book to make sense of it all.

The March sisters never stray too far or too long from home. But they do know a good deal about change and its bittersweet harvests: loss, renewal, joy, grief, evolution. As a woman with one foot in the East and another in the West, I find that one March sister in particular seems to embody the contradictions and complexities of being: Amy. In my eyes, Vevay is now pivotal to *Little Women* as the place that, beneath its peaceful vistas, crackles with tension. I suspect Amy does not ease into her happy ending as smoothly as that boat glides through the water at noon. Rather, her happiness is the fruit of decades of painful and exhilarating character growth. From white satin slippers to silk tulle to the iconic illusion, it's no coincidence that Amy is earmarked for Alcott's richest cosmetic descriptions. She herself is a ball gown trimmed over and over, embracing a thousand and one snips to become who she wants to be.

A crucial caveat before I launch my love letter to Amy: I'm aware that *Little Women* has been lambasted for its unrelenting focus on women's emotional labor. Feminist critics have thoughtfully argued that the March sisters are poked and prodded into rigid straitjackets of femininity. While agreeing, I venture to raise one important point: Alcott's didactic writing style means that *no* central character, whether man or woman, escapes the pressure to change on moral grounds. Hence, while paying tribute to Amy's constant drive for self-improvement, I don't see her as a woman trying to squeeze herself into oppressive boxes. I see her as a craftswoman (of art, self, and life) brimming with ambition and perseverance.

At university, I decided to plunge into nonprofit work, which meant engaging deeply, sometimes heart-wrenchingly, with the reality of global poverty. It transformed the way I read *Little Women*. The very first time we meet Amy, she laments how "I don't think it's fair for some girls to have plenty of pretty things, and other girls nothing at all." Her lament reminds me of little girls from low-income families I volunteer with in Mumbai. Like Amy, these little girls confess their yearning for a better life with the innocent forthrightness of childhood, despite being reminded of their poverty by more world-weary adults. I think that in any other book, Amy's might have been an unremarkable and perfectly understandable statement. In Alcott's world of elevated expectations for moral conduct, however, a twelve-year-old's longing for pretty things symbolizes sinful vanity. From the clothespin on her nose to excess lobster, Amy is lampooned for her frivolity throughout the series. As much as I love Alcott, I find my adult self questioning these authorial choices.

At any given time, I am either in England, Singapore or India. This means being either ensconced in the affluence of a first-world country, or confronted with the suffering of a developing one. From Cambridge's May Balls to Mumbai's child beggars, I have been starkly exposed to inequalities between the rich and the poor. When I read *Little Women* now, I reflect on what poverty actually means. Alcott does not dwell on the sisters' privations beyond depicting their lack of fine dresses and parties as lessons in humility and simplicity. But now, I wonder about the untold stories in the March household. Did Meg ever go to bed hungry? Did Jo ever have to skip school to help with the housework? Would Beth have survived with costlier, better medical care? The more I reflect on uncomfortable, yet highly plausible, gaps in the narrative, the more sympathy I feel for Amy. She is universally shamed for her "mercenary" desire to marry a rich man. Yet, trapped in an era that would have granted her little chance of independently attaining financial security, perhaps Amy can be forgiven for trying to forge a pragmatic path out of poverty? Her relentless striving to be a "gentlewoman" does not seem snobbish as much as it does aspirational. Amy ultimately wants a life where she doesn't worry about scraping up enough money just to buy limes, and I think that's okay.

In our interconnected twenty-first century, where the hardships of human beings around the globe are only ever an internet headline away, I find myself probing the cross-cultural implications of my sympathy for Amy. In some ways, her positioning as a white woman in New England gives her yards more privilege than the vulnerable citizens of the developing world. Nevertheless, I wonder whether a literary character deserves to be chastised just for daring to dream of escaping a life of deprivation. We live in an age where boundaries are blurring. We're constantly bumping up against people on different rungs of the socioeconomic ladder. Empathy and compassion have never been so necessary. Amy is one of the few *Little Women* characters who lets slip that poverty is not always a beautiful, edifying pathway to self-actualization. So the sight of her enjoying the luxurious beauty around her in that boat in Vevey—and becoming financially stable as a happy by-product of her romance—makes me glad.

As I shuttle back and forth between countries, I'm also inspired by the subtler nuances of Amy's character. Amy doesn't have Jo's firecracker charm or Meg's domestic appeal or Beth's saintly pathos, but she does have the quiet heroism of everyday self-restraint and sacrifice. As I wait in line to board planes and will myself not to wilt on sixteen-hour flights, I marvel at her patience. Taking the time to chat politely to old ladies, paying six calls in a row, sitting for hours at a lonely flower table in the corner—Amy's little triumphs of spirit aren't mundane. They're mighty. As an international student who constantly endures airport security checks, lugs heavy bags on her own and contends with the infinite frustrations of moving house, I know how difficult, yet rewarding, it can be to stay patient and good-humored. Through Amy, Alcott seems to champion the art of navigating everyday life with grace.

Most compellingly, Amy evokes, for me, the power of growth. I'm currently embarking on another new beginning as I prepare to move from England to the United States. Amy reassures me that it's okay to change. Out of all four sisters, her journey looks the most like an arc. Initially, she's a little self-absorbed—can't you just picture a modern preteen Amy Photoshopping her Instagram selfies and deleting Jo's blog in a fit of temper?

But older Amy comes into her own. Some of her self-realizations resonate with me. Cambridge is often seen as a bastion of privilege; people debate the value allegedly placed on 'posh' accents and private school education. As students, most of us want things to change and become fairer, more inclusive. Perhaps our twenty-first century world seems radically different from Amy's, but really, we're questioning the very same class structures that tempt her to snub a grocery man's son. So I cheer when Amy finally stops equating social status with superiority. I also find it poignant when she gracefully relinquishes her artistic aspirations. I, too, had to surrender my childhood dream of being a writer in order to enter the nonprofit sector. Adulthood entails compromise. But, as Amy shows, there are compensations. Her arc is threaded with constant redemption. As she bounces back from disappointment—the disastrous charcoal painting, the thwarted party for twelve, the discovery that she isn't a genius—Amy personifies resilience and elasticity. The considerate, self-possessed woman we see at Vevay is eons away from the mildly spoilt child at the start of *Little Women*. I thus conclude that she fully deserves her "pretty little tableau of human love and happiness." Amy hasn't lived in as many places as I have, but she's travelled further.

---

## About the Author

---

***Nomisha C. Kurian*** is an MPhil student undertaking the 2017–18 Education, Globalization and International Development degree at the University of Cambridge. She researches global poverty and issues of wellbeing in developing countries. Previously, she undertook the 2014-2017 BA in Education at the University of Cambridge and has worked with charities in India and England. She is the 2018-19 recipient of the Henry Fellowship to Yale where she hopes to take a few literature classes and read more Alcott novels! Her favorite possession is the dog-eared, yellowing, much-read and much-loved copy of *Little Women* on her bedside table.

# At Home with Meg March

*by Donna Macdonald*

ᔓᔕ

I first read *Little Women* when I was nine years old. My book, given to me by mother, was a quaint 1960s edition with several lyrical illustrations. I was especially drawn to images of pretty Meg—she is the one quietly folding Marmee's scarf in the background and packing the trunk that would take the sisters' mother away to Washington, D.C., to tend to their sick father. With the help of the book's images, I also idealized the budding romance between Meg and Mr. Brooke. Meg's quiet, helpful ways and tender courtship made an impression on me and I came to realize that she was everything I wanted to be when I grew up.

While most girls who read *Little Women* immediately align with Jo, I adored Meg and felt she got short shrift. At first glance, she may indeed seem the least interesting of the March sisters with mistress-of-herself and scene-stealing Jo, dear and sweet Beth, and artistic and haughty 'baby' sister, Amy. But if you give yourself a chance to know Meg, you see that still waters run deep and there is much to love about her soft and feminine ways.

As I grew and read and re-read *Little Women* over and over again, rose-sprigged Meg and her love of pretty things reminded me of myself. She wasn't ashamed to admit that she wanted a new fashionable dress or some other lovely thing. She announced her desires out loud, even during a crushing wartime. A one-time social climber, Meg settled into a life of domesticity and eventually chose true love over money. She was yin to Jo's yang, a domestic doyenne to Jo's free-spirited tomboy.

Maybe my love for Meg stems from being always at my grandmother's knee, a real-life Martha Stewart before 'Martha' existed, where I was taught all the old-fashioned Victorian ways of keeping house such as ironing sheets and swatting at carpets outdoors. And as my grandmother's attentive pupil, I also learned that there was nothing wrong with wanting to be 'just' a wife who tends a house and the people in it. As time went by, my grandmother's teachings settled upon me like a warm handknit shawl, and like Meg, I wanted to find my Mr. Brooke and make a home for him.

In many ways, Meg is the bravest little woman—even braver than Jo and Amy, whose passions took them far afield to find their destinies. In a household filled with Marmee's feminist concepts and a sister who lived them out in front of her, courageous Meg chose a subtler path and made no apologies for it. Neither did I on the day I set out to find my own Mr. Brooke. And like Meg, I have joyfully and bravely tended our home fires.

## About the Author

***Donna Macdonald*** is a freelance writer who covers style, fashion, motherhood, and careers. She is a regular contributor for *Fairygodboss* and wrote material for a best seller that netted her an appearance on *The Oprah Winfrey Show*. You can find her regularly on her blog, *A Lovely Inconsequence*, where she writes about the things that touch a woman's heart.

# Apollyon on Thin Ice

*by Julie Dunlap*

ᔓ

Steel blades bite into the frozen Concord River in my favorite scene from *Little Women*. Each sister races her own demons across the ice, cheeks burning in the cold, hearts thumping with exertion and fury. But the chapter title, "Jo Meets Apollyon," leaves no doubt who faces the greater peril. A fish-scaled, fire-breathing dragon named Apollyon menaced the hero in my parents' illustrated *Pilgrim's Progress*, and as a child I shuddered in dread of the terrors he posed for my heroine. Then—crack!—the Concord's surface splits, plunging Amy into the icy waters, and Jo into despair.

The next scene is a blur of frantic reactions: a traumatized Jo failing to summon help, yet help arriving in the form of Laurie's cool head and strong arms. Swaddled in the cloaks of her rescuers, a sodden Amy is carried home and tucked in by the fire, her petulant chatter stilled for once with shock and maybe a little gratitude. I remember thinking—petulant myself at times—that Amy deserved her dousing. As a tetchy pre-teen with horse stories accumulating in my private drawer, I could conceive of no sin exceeding the destruction of Jo's fairytale manuscript.

If my little brother had burned my notebooks, he'd have faced hotter wrath than steaming soup by a crackling blaze.

Did I skim past Marmee's moral of the misadventure, on the necessity of taming what Jo calls her "dreadful temper"? As often as I have re-read that chapter, Mrs. March's words still ring unfamiliar: "Watch and pray, dear, never get tired of trying, and never think it is impossible to conquer your fault." Maybe they jarred against my predilection, that her admonitions belonged to Amy for her frippery, not Jo with her literary ambitions, or what Alcott called her vision splendid.

Unlike Jo, when Louisa May Alcott admitted her vices, she listed not swift anger but "inordinate love of cats." It took years and a few biographies for me to distinguish between the author and her creation, and to realize I shared a passion beyond words with the former. Who wouldn't fall in love with nature, as Louisa did, on her childhood field trips led by Henry Thoreau? Huckleberry parties and rowing on Walden Pond brought her essential relief from indoor chores and Bronson Alcott's Transcendental strictures, and Thoreau (who skated figure eights on the Concord with Nathaniel Hawthorne and Ralph Waldo Emerson) taught the duty-bound girl that freedom and wildness often mean the same thing.

I trained as a wildlife ecologist rather than a writer, but often try to share my inordinate love of nature by writing articles and books, for children and adults. My first picture book celebrated Louisa's childhood friendship with Henry Thoreau. Their joyous connection puts the lie to images of Thoreau as a curmudgeonly misanthrope, warm to foxes and goshawks but cool to fellow Concordians. Henry led the Alcott girls to pick huckleberries, taught Louisa to see dewy spider webs as fairy handkerchiefs, and played the flute with the family beside Walden Pond. Was Louisa thinking of their tramps in the wood, or of digging in Henry's melon patch, when she sent Jo's little men to roam around Plumfield, or assigned them each a garden? "It takes so little to make a child happy," says Jo Bhaer, "that it is a pity in a world full of sunshine and pleasant things, that there should be any wistful faces, empty hands, or lonely little hearts."

Wonders of the seasons, the earth and the sky, must have meant still more to an aging Louisa, living with physical pain and the losses of a cherished mother and two sisters. I trust she relied on Henry's sustaining lessons and shared them with May's orphaned daughter. Surely she led Lulu by the hand to follow rabbit tracks in snow or discover the closest stream for splashing. "We live in a beautiful and wonderful world," Louisa may have assured Lulu, as Jo does Demi, "and the more you know about it, the wiser and better you will become."

Yet knowing the world's splendors could not prevent thunderclouds darkening Alcott's moods, or mine. For Louisa, flares threatened when household drudgery, filial duties, or financial burdens constrained her freedom to create. In my case, news of vanishing flora and fauna, the most permanent kind of biological loss, sets me to boil. Decades in conservation work have not inured me to the ravages of deforestation, pollution, and overfishing. I seek solace in occasional successes—bald eagles saved from DDT, bison grazing again on the Great Plains—and in tireless leaders like Jane Goodall and E.O. Wilson, who fight with passion and civility, no matter what calumnies opponents of their message hurl their way. If a critic challenges Wilson with, "What difference does one kind of beetle make, more or less?" he will explain over and again why the pageant of evolution has produced 400,000 equally precious forms of Coleoptera. But while generations have listened to Marmee persuade Amy that her bonfire inflicted upon Jo a permanent loss, few seem to hear Wilson's warning of the perils of biological extinction: "This is the folly our descendants are least likely to forgive us."

Freed by absolving Amy, Jo tames her anger over the course of three novels. Louisa seemed to master hers enough to write prolifically, under two names, despite chronic pain and family obligations. In contrast, my outbursts seem to multiply, as the pace of species loss accelerates. In geological timescales, extinctions can be 'natural,' at an estimated rate of one to five species per year. But ecologists say we currently face a global mass extinction, a rare event when dozens of species disappear weekly, at a rate 1,000-fold greater than normal. Whole families of animals are in peril, including the wild versions of Louisa's beloved cats. Palm oil plantations threaten Sumatran tigers, poaching may wipe out Cambodia's leopards, and vehicle collisions likely will doom Florida panthers. By 2050, the only African lions left may resemble the stone versions guarding the March neighbors' mansion. Grief and, yes, rage seem appropriate responses to such heedless destruction. Even serene Meg, helpless to rescue Beth from crushing illness, laments, "I wish I had no heart, it aches so."

Heart-sore ecologists know the crisis is deepened by climate change. Hotter, drier rainforests burn, consuming jaguar habitat. Melting glaciers open alpine habitat to livestock, squeezing snow leopards out. Some of the most poignant evidence comes from Concord, where Thoreau collected meticulous records of natural phenomena starting in 1851. Thanks to Henry, we know the area's mean annual temperature has climbed 4.5 degrees Fahrenheit, and insects, birds, frogs, trees, and flowers are struggling to cope. With flowering dates shifting as much as three weeks earlier, plants may not bloom in synchrony with their pollinators' spring arrival, and fail in their essential task of setting seed. Some organisms are more resilient than others, but hardest-hit species include dogwoods, orchids, lilies, and violets—wild cousins of flowers Jo calls "heart's ease." Would Henry and Louisa recognize the altered landscape of Concord? Twenty-seven percent of the plants in Thoreau's notebooks are now absent, and 36% so rare that extinction appears imminent. The seasons that stand for rebirth and hope in their journals and books are fundamentally changed. Surely anger would be one of the emotions the friends would experience in the transformed woodlands. But I can still imagine an irrepressible Henry bending over young Louisa, small hands achingly empty of violets. "There is no remedy for love," he would assure her, "but to love more."

I long believed that anger should drive my activism. Railing against the greed, indifference, and impoverished imaginations that drive extinction, I thought, would spark change, as in *Pilgrim's Progress* when Evangeline's scroll of doom warns Christian onto the straight and narrow path. Sometimes my outrage seemed pure, almost crystalline; who could deny its power? But thinking of Louisa's Apollyon gives me pause. It's not her burden of temper we remember, but her shining ideals, embodied in the loyal and loving March family, and in the Alcotts themselves. In her courage and devotion to a cause—supporting her loved ones—Louisa reminds me again of my favorite conservationists. Jane Goodall without doubt sometimes rages at the diminishment of her treasured Gombe National Park. At 83, she writes, travels, and speaks to anyone who will listen about the urgency of wildlife protection and climate action. Anger can be her tool, as when Goodall blasted U.S. withdrawal from the Paris Agreement, undeterred by climate-fueled hurricanes Harvey and Maria. But far from demonizing her opponents, she strives to share with them her glory in the nature that remains, and her dream of a still more beautiful, rebounding tomorrow. Love is the power behind her persistence. Like Louisa, my conservation heroes realize that fits of temper are unreliable energy sources. Deep attachment, to people, places, and the living world, offers enduring consolation and uplifting hope.

For 150 years, *Little Women* readers have been captivated by Louisa's vision of a harmonious family, nurturing enough to set each member splendidly free. Apollyons of temper, revenge, and, today, the growing uncertainty of spring, offer only temporary obstacles along the way. I too need a clear-eyed view of the future, one that accepts undeniable loss while appreciating the wondrous abundance that remains. I can never fully tame my tempests, and I will fall as if through thin ice. But I will rise again to emulate Louisa in steering a truer, more bounteous course. And like my heroine, I hope someday to proclaim, "I'm not afraid of storms, for I'm learning how to sail my ship."

## About the Author

***Julie Dunlap*** teaches wildlife ecology and environmental science at the University of Maryland University College. She has written and edited numerous articles, essays, and books, including *Louisa May and Mr. Thoreau's Flute* (with Marybeth Lorbiecki), *Janey Monarch Seed* (forthcoming) and *Coming of Age at the End of Nature: A Generation Faces Living on a Changed Planet* (edited with Susan A. Cohen). She earned a PhD in social ecology from Yale University, and serves on the boards of the Audubon Society of Central Maryland and of the Community Ecology Institute.

# Dollanity

*by Rachel Roberts*

❧

*"There were six dolls to be taken up and dressed every morning, for Beth was a child still, and loved her pets as well as ever."*

—"Burdens," *Little Women*

A few months ago I gave into a hankering I'd held for a while and bought myself a doll. The Barbie I named Sarah is a 'curvy' from the *Fashionistas* range whose debut had prompted feminist interest as their varying body shapes and racial features supposedly represented the diversity of real women. Aside, they are still pretty and Western beauty standards remain intact.

Soon after, Sarah acquired an Instagram account (Leeds_Barbie). I didn't have any other accounts and Sarah would allow me to share cultural and scenic highlights of my area (Leeds, UK) in a fun and relatively anonymous way. Sarah now frequently ventures out in public with me.

Subsequently, I have found a thriving online community of adults who like dolls. Many are collectors, yet others, like me, enjoy the more childlike activities of dressing them and creating personalities and stories. Similar to Beth March, many have an impulse to rescue and restore toys, the most viral example being *Tree Change Dolls* where Australian Sonia Singh turns discarded Bratz into more natural-looking schoolgirls. I have taken to checking the previously uninteresting toy section of charity shops in search of new clothes for Sarah, which are surprisingly expensive and hard to come by new. Like/unlike Beth, I don't keep up with my dolls' sewing because stitching seams is boring. I have acquired some more dolls just for their clothes. There is something unsavory about sending them back to join the pile of naked bodies in a secondhand store, so Sarah has been joined by friends Dolores and Lexy.

Although many would view our pastime as childish, the market for children's toys for adults is growing as a new generation, often with greater disposable income than their parents, looks for escapism and self-expression. Meanwhile, many children lose interest in playing with traditional toys as young as seven. We assume that in the time of *Little Women*, with fewer electronic amusements, youngsters would have retained their toys until an older age. Beth (aged thirteen) would be classed as a teenager to us, but is described as a little girl. Meg, Jo, Beth and Amy portray the strange duality of girls in the nineteenth century, occupying themselves with seemingly childish activities such as playacting while they are expected to take on employment and housekeeping and compete on the marriage market.

Coming of age is a major theme in *Little Women* and Beth is frequently cited as the sister with the least development. Alcott introduces her to us as an innocent whose best friends are dolls and kittens, a girl who retains an air of unworldliness into adulthood. Some readers have even interpreted Beth to have a degree of learning disability, although I believe there is little to support this.

Like her sisters, Beth is resourceful. There are frequent references to the "ragbag." As a middle-class family under financial strain, the thrifty Marches collect old cloth to exchange for pocket money. Textiles were reused (Amy is in receipt of cousin Flo's tasteless hand-me-downs) and refashioned and then traded down to the poorest before being reduced to rags. Increasing prices during the American Civil War (due to shortages of material and labor) would have led to an even greater recycling in this way. Meg and Amy are adept fashion upcyclers—Meg salvages (badly fitting) shoes, presumably donated by affluent neighbors, to wear at a party. In her quiet way, Beth joins in this pastime of budget fashion. "An assortment of doll's millinery" is mentioned in the sisters' Pickwick Portfolio, presumably items made from scraps. When Meg goes to *Vanity Fair*, there are several references to her being treated as a doll, a pretty thing which (wealthier) girls dress up and then discard. In contrast, Beth's play is based around her dolls being hapless children whose needs she must serve, an unusual game even given the poor state of repair of her toys. We see she possesses empathy for the vulnerable and disadvantaged, yet her "bosom enemy," chronic shyness, has prevented her from attending school and venturing beyond home. Through adopting imaginary friends, is Beth rehearsing the social interactions which will allow her to take her skills to those in need? After all, Beth goes on to befriend lonely Mr. Laurence and risk her life assisting an impoverished immigrant family.

Unlike our own times where 'kidults' (myself included) curate figurines, doll-playing is firmly associated with childhood in *Little Women*. In Volume I, little Beth uses play to recreate and explore the adult world. There is no mention of her dolls in Volume II and we see older Beth take on the burden of attempting to shield her family from her declining health and, even when terminally ill, continue to knit and sew for the poor.

Critics sometimes regard Beth's early death as a lazy literary device, a means of disposing of a character too inadequate to grow up and join society, by transforming her into the popular Victorian archetype of the angelic invalid. However, Alcott includes several gentle suggestions of potential romances for Beth—for instance, Frank Vaughn and later, Laurie. Her games may suggest a maternal nature which is ultimately unfilled. In the final chapters, Alcott includes a passage on the value of aunts within a family, and many readers would be satisfied with an ending where Beth lived on and devoted herself to her parents, sisters and their children. Rather than an inevitable fate, Beth's demise is a poignant and premature death of a nurturing, sensitive woman yet to realize her full potential.

---

## About the Author

---

***Rachel Roberts*** grew up in Leeds, England. She studied English literature at Newcastle University and lived for a time in Scotland. She currently lives in Leeds with her partner and works in housing. Rachel enjoys running and posting about cross stitch design and dolls.

# *Little Women*, Feminism, and a New Definition of Beauty

*by Lauren Cutrone*

ℭ

*"Dear me, let us be elegant or die!"*

—"The Laurence Boy," *Little Women*

Women are subjected rather unfairly to a substantial amount of advertising. Whether it be via magazines or billboards or commercials, the need to be young, taut, and ravishingly beautiful is everywhere. Though the self-love movement is beginning to step up and take its rightful place, those ads still exist everywhere you go. Even the most strong-willed of women find it difficult to resist. Beauty, we're told, is power. And what woman doesn't want to be powerful?

There's nothing wrong with giving in to those ads every so often. I myself do it more than I like to admit. Though I have more lipstick than I ever plan on using, the temptation to purchase more always strikes me. The problem with these ads, however, is the insinuation that all of life's problems can be solved by a simple application of mascara. So long as one has access to beauty products, personality and intelligence do not matter.

It wasn't until I went to college that someone told me otherwise. I'm still not entirely sure what had inspired me to sign up for a class in the women's and gender studies department. Before that class, I didn't think that was something you *could* study. Feminism, I had been taught by society, was bad. To be a feminist meant to be severe and unfriendly and—perhaps worst of all to a twenty-year-old woman—unattractive. So I crossed over that divide hesitantly, taking a class in the subject as sort of a trial run.

Though I was unsure, I opened myself up to the possibilities that the class had to offer and found that it changed me with each passing day. I met a sisterhood in that classroom, a group of women with whom I could confide my deepest feminist beliefs. We all held a fury deep within ourselves that, until that moment, we were unable to share with anyone else. Our feelings were validated, we were taught. We were angry over the mistreatment of women and we had every right to be.

But a moment of realization came when my professor stood in front of the class and said something that confused me, something that I had previously never heard said out loud:

"It is not your job as a woman to be beautiful for someone else."

She was right, of course. I knew she was right. But to hear someone verbalize it with so much confidence and certainty frightened me.

It took me time to struggle with her words. But ultimately, every time I tried to argue with her assessment of a woman's role in the world, I ended unsuccessful. I had already known her words to be true, even if I had never heard them said to me before.

I knew them to be true because Louisa May Alcott's *Little Women* had always told me so.

*Little Women* carries so many lessons, but one that I valued above all others was the message that it doesn't take curled hair and rouged cheeks and a closet full of dresses to be beautiful. No, rather it's the soul of a woman that makes her beautiful. It's her mind and heart and willingness to help others in need that make her truly lovely.

In Louisa May Alcott's coming-of-age story of sisterhood and love, we are introduced to the March family and very quickly see a scene at Christmas breakfast. It isn't often the girls have a special meal, even on a holiday as significant as Christmas. And yet Marmee, wanting to impart this message that kindness influences beauty, asks her daughters to consider sacrificing their delicious meal for a poor German family who has nothing at all. Though it's a difficult decision, the girls give up their food eagerly, impatient to assist a family in need. From the start, Marmee teaches her daughters that to give is to be beautiful. To love another without any expectation of reciprocation—*that* is what it means to be lovely.

Meg nearly forgets this lesson. Just as I tried on the persona of a feminist, Meg dressed as a woman of society at a coming out party at the Moffats'. She drinks champagne and allows the girls to dress her up and finds pleasure in such frivolity. But when she sees a familiar face in Laurie, she feels shame over her behavior. Once she returns home, she confesses:

> "I told you they dressed me up, but I didn't tell you that they powdered and squeezed and frizzled, and made me look a fashion plate. Laurie thought I wasn't proper, I know he did, though he didn't say so, and one man called me 'a doll.' I knew it was silly, but they flattered me and said I was a beauty, and quantities of nonsense, so I let them make a fool of me."

Marmee doesn't judge her daughter for what she confesses:

> "That is perfectly natural, and quite harmless, if the liking does not become a passion and lead one to do foolish or unmaidenly things. Learn to know and value the praise which is worth having, and to excite the admiration of excellent people by being modest as well as pretty, Meg."

It is a lesson the girls carry with them for the rest of the books in the *Little Women* series and it is a lesson that sits with me each day as well. It is all right to enjoy the sensation of feeling pretty to others. But to abandon everything about yourself that makes you good and thoughtful towards others for the pursuit of that standard of beauty, Marmee says, is unforgivable.

My professor, a bit like Marmee herself, believed the same. She led me to understand a truth about myself that I hadn't yet realized—despite my doubts, I had always been a feminist, believing first in the capabilities of women before their aesthetics. Beauty was a wonderful thing to have but prettiness fades. The inner workings of our minds, however, last forever and can guard us against injustice and cruelty. *Little Women* had raised me to believe such things and my professor reminded me of those very lessons that Louisa was writing so progressively in 1868.

I'm sure that my loved ones are eternally tired of my prattling on about *Little Women* and all that Louisa May Alcott has given me. But to me, *Little Women* isn't just a story about a family of women in Concord. Instead, this story was instrumental in shaping who I have become and who I have always been. From the time I was a young girl, Louisa May Alcott gave me permission to be a kind, courteous, outspoken, thinking woman in a society that was otherwise unforgiving. And so long as I have her words, I will always feel beautiful.

## About the Author

***Lauren Cutrone*** is a writer and publishing professional located in New Jersey. She has been a fan of Alcott's work since she was a child and has been a member of the Louisa May Alcott Society for five years. In her spare time, she is a reader, a blogger, a baker, photographer, an avid tea drinker, and a dog enthusiast. Her bookish ramblings can be read at *Hooray for YA*.

# Growing Up Catholic with *Little Women:* The Mystery of the Rosary

*by Stephanie A. Mann*

ຜ

Like many other readers of *Little Women*, I nearly memorized the book when I was maturing. The memory of one passage has stayed with me through the years. It stunned me when I was growing up—growing up Catholic, attending Catholic schools, meditating on the mysteries of the Rosary, venerating the saints, going to Mass—living in a Catholic milieu (as I do today).

When Beth is ill with scarlet fever, and Marmee is nursing Mr. March back to health in Washington, Amy is sent to stay with Aunt March and has a trying time. Esther, Aunt March's French maid, is the only person who pays much attention to Amy. Esther changed her name from Estelle at Madame's request but ruled out any change in her religious observance: Esther is a Catholic.

Esther shows Amy her aunt's jewelry as a way to entertain the girl. As they discuss the jewelry, the issue of religion comes up when Amy selects one piece for special admiration:

> "Which would Mademoiselle choose if she had her will?" asked Esther, who always sat near to watch over and lock up the valuables.
>
> "I like the diamonds best, but there is no necklace among them, and I'm fond of necklaces, they are so becoming. I should choose this if I might," replied Amy, looking with great admiration at a string of gold and ebony beads from which hung a heavy cross of the same.
>
> "I, too, covet that, but not as a necklace. Ah, no! To me it is a rosary, and as such I should use it like a good Catholic," said Esther, eyeing the handsome thing wistfully.

Amy has seen Esther's rosary and has also noticed a difference in prayerful Esther:

> "You seem to take a great deal of comfort in your prayers, Esther, and always come down looking quiet and satisfied. I wish I could."
>
> "If Mademoiselle was a Catholic, she would find true comfort, but as that is not to be, it would be well if you went apart each day to meditate and pray, as did the good mistress whom I served before Madame. She had a little chapel, and in it found solacement for much trouble."

Amy does need some solace beyond Laurie's visits, so she agrees to Esther creating a little chapel. Esther includes a copy of a famous painting of "the Divine

Mother" whom I always knew as Mary, the Mother of God, the Blessed Virgin Mary and even another rosary. Amy makes her own additions to her prayer closet:

> On the table she laid her little testament and hymnbook, kept a vase always full of the best flowers Laurie brought her, and came every day to "sit alone thinking good thoughts, and praying the dear God to preserve her sister." Esther had given her a rosary of black beads with a silver cross, but Amy hung it up and did not use it, feeling doubtful as to its fitness for Protestant prayers.

This passage awakened my sense of Catholic identity. Where the March girls read John Bunyan's *Pilgrim's Progress*, I read Thomas a Kempis' *Imitation of Christ*; where the March family helped the poor Germans in their hometown, I saved nickels for the missions to help poor starving children in Africa. I knew, of course, that there are many differences between Protestants and Catholics in doctrine and practice. My father, who became a Catholic when I was in high school, was raised in a Protestant family, so I had aunts and uncles who attended either the Church of God or the Methodist church. Some of them were more anti-Catholic—that is, convinced we were going to Hell—than others, but familial bonds of love were essential and we all got along very well.

Nevertheless, Amy March—and Aunt March, evidently, since it was in her "Indian cabinet, full of queer drawers, little pigeonholes, and secret places"—thinking that a rosary was a necklace shocked me. And why did Aunt March even *have* a rosary? Did she buy it on a trip to Europe? Perhaps her husband bought it for her because it was beautiful and they had never thought of it as a religious object, a sacramental as Esther knew it was.

And I was fascinated by Esther/Estelle: I wondered how she maintained her Catholic faith as a servant in a Protestant household. Where did she go to Mass? Was she allowed time off to attend Mass every Sunday and on Holy Days of Obligation? Was she permitted to abstain from meat and fowl as required on Fridays? Aunt March allowed her some free time in the home to pray and meditate, but how free was she to practice her faith? Although Esther "rather tyrannized over the old lady" Aunt March "could not get along without her" so perhaps they had reached a compromise.

I knew that colonial Massachusetts had been settled by anti-Catholic Puritans and Congregationalists; Catholic priests were not permitted in the colony at all (and Christmas wasn't celebrated for many years, either). From 1780 until 1834, the citizens of Massachusetts did not have freedom of religion; local Congregational parishes received tax support, and state office holders had to swear an oath that they were Protestant. Because Catholics had been generally supportive of the cause of independence from Great Britain, however, they were slowly accepted in Massachusetts and the other colonies. Many Protestant benefactors, including John Adams, contributed to the establishment of the first cathedral in Boston in 1808.

In turn, many Irish Catholics in Massachusetts served in the Union Army during the Civil War (around 10,000)—German and Polish Catholics from the North did also—so Mr. March might have met some during his service. Immigrant Catholics wanted to prove their loyalty to the United States of America and shed their blood to do so.

By the 1960s and 1970s, of course, in part because of the Kennedy family, Catholicism and Massachusetts were closely associated, but in the era of Alcott's *Little Women*, Catholics were still alien and aroused suspicion because they were different.

I thought about the name Aunt March had selected for her French maid: Esther, an Old Testament biblical name. Martin Luther doubted the value of the Book of Esther and certain passages in it that are found in the Catholic Vulgate Bible aren't in most Protestant Bibles. The story of Esther is of a Hebrew woman who becomes the Queen of Persia and saves the Jews in Persia from the genocide planned by Haman. A French Catholic in a Protestant household accepts the name of a Jewish girl in a Persian court! Raised as I was after the Second Vatican Council, my Catholic school education included Bible studies, looking at the historical sources and discussing methods of interpretation, so I recognized the irony of Alcott's choice of name for Aunt March's maid.

While Esther knew that it was not her place to try to convert Amy, she did not apologize for thinking her Catholic faith superior to Amy's Protestant religion. And she placed a set of rosary beads in the prayer closet she arranged for the "young pilgrim." Like Esther in the Old Testament, Aunt March's French maid is willing to stand up for her faith. Whenever I had to explain some Catholic practice to non-Catholic family members or neighbors—and prayer to Mary and the saints, or the 'vain repetition' of the Rosary were common subjects—I think Esther inspired me to be confident and not defensive; positive and not pushy.

As I continued to read Louisa May Alcott's other books, I noticed other references to Catholic themes. *Rose in Bloom* offers two particularly rich examples, with the extended discussion by Rose and Charlie of the merits of saints like St. Francis of Assisi and St. Martin of Tours and Mac's view of Rose as a Correggio Madonna.

The mystery of the rosary in Aunt March's Indian cabinet inspired me to understand the faith into which I had been born, my Church's history in the United States, and how to defend the doctrines and devotions of Catholicism.

I think that Alcott would be surprised.

## About the Author

***Stephanie A. Mann*** is a Wichita, Kansas, author and presenter who has carved out a niche as a specialist on the English Reformation and historical apologetics for national Catholic media like EWTN TV and Radio, *The National Catholic Register*, OSV's *The Catholic Answer Magazine*, *Homiletic & Pastoral Review*, *Crisis Magazine*, *Catholic World Report*, and *The Saint Austin Review*. She also writes often for *Tudor Life*, the publication of the Tudor Society. Her book, *Supremacy and Survival: How Catholics Endured the English Reformation*, is available from Scepter Publishers. She blogs at *Supremacy and Survival: The English Reformation*.

# My Beth

*by Verena Demel*

❧

Some people might call Elizabeth March a Mary Sue, a boring, saintly, perfect girl. They say that they're glad she died before they died of boredom.

But this is my story. A story explaining why I'm annoyed by such comments. A story about Beth, one of my favorite literary characters. A story that started in Germany.

It began when I got to school for the first time and received a book with abridged illustrated classics. *Little Women—Kleine Frauen*—was a part of the book, which included the Christmas chapter. I only knew this story, and Beth intrigued me.

I asked the local bookseller if she had *Kleine Frauen* but she didn't know it, so *Little Women* was still a mystery. It remained so until I bought a combo DVD with *Sense and Sensibility* and a movie called *Betty und ihre Schwestern* ("Betty and her Sisters"), a classic set during the American Civil War. This was the full description. Even though the sisters looked very different from my illustrations, I opened the DVD case and saw the English title: *Little Women.*

Before watching the film, I bought the book *Betty und ihre Schwestern* and I loved it. It was a German translation, ending with a chapter called "Tante March und die Liebe." How well it ended! Meg and John got engaged! Jo and Laurie kissed! And Beth/Betty had such an impressive role that the book was named after her. I was blissfully happy.

Then I watched my DVD. That was the turning point. Jo and Laurie didn't kiss, and worse than that—

Beth died.

It was the most horrible day in my literary life. My Beth, oh, my dear Beth! I double checked the story. The movie, not my book, was correct.

Curious, I searched for different translations, old and new versions, finding different European editions (*Piccole Donne*, *Mujercitas*, *Les quatre filles du Docteur March*), as well as film variants, to see how Beth's story and character both change.

I learned that most international editions either cut Volume II (what we know as *Good Wives*) completely or publish it as its own book. Also, Beth's physical look differs significantly in illustrated editions: sometimes she is a pale girl with ginger hair, and sometimes a rosy girl with smooth black hair. I found one edition with Jo and Laurie marrying and Beth surviving, a retelling by Pascale Vanoverschelde. In one movie, *The March Sisters at Christmas*, Beth is a sweet background character who becomes a music teacher. Beth becomes the heroine in Claudia Salvatori's graphic novel *Piccole Papere* ("Little Ducks"). In this Italian parody, a good-hearted but strong-minded Beth encourages her sisters to be helpful and invents the teabag. This Beth was neither a musician nor an invalid—and she didn't die.

And so I asked myself: What would have happened if Beth had survived?

Jo wouldn't have written a poem called "My Beth." Friedrich wouldn't have found Jo's poem "In the Garret," realized her loneliness, and come back. Amy wouldn't have grieved, and Laurie wouldn't have returned to her. Wasn't grief the reason why Jo started longing for love and becoming a better woman? Didn't her sister's death inspire Jo to write about her life?

In all these years of my Beth-quest, I have recognized that Beth is more than a celestial guide, as Aslauga was for Dan in *Jo's Boys.* Beth isn't boring. She has her fears, she works, she struggles with shyness, but she is the strongest sister. She keeps her anxiety and pain a secret, and guides her sisters, even if separated. How touching is the scene in which Jo thanks her sister in the end of the movie from 1933! Or the hopeful rainbow in the movie from 1949?

I think about the different translations and outcomes of the foreign editions of *Little Women.* There is a reason we keep trying to revise and retell Beth's story.

Beth is still guiding us together on our own *Pilgrim's Progress.*

## About the Author

***Verena Demel***, born in 1996, loves writing stories, poems and plays. However, like Beth, she has always been too bashful even to talk about her creative work. She followed Jo's steps by studying education at the Ludwig Maximilian University of Munich, Germany, since 2014. Verena's work is dedicated mostly to *Little Women.*

# "I Call You Friend"—Louisa May Alcott as Muse, Guide and Grief Counselor

*by Susan Bailey*

ೞ

*I call you friend,*
*though you lived long before me*
*It's your words, your wisdom shining through.*

*The stories told of the losses and heartache,*
*of triumphs and the hope that make me want to be like you.*

*And now I find your spirit in the pen on the page,*
*You've become my muse, my guide, my sage.*

*I will remember you …*[1]

Louisa May Alcott has been a part of my life since I was nine years old, but I had to grow up with the author first before I could fully appreciate her coming-of-age classic, *Little Women.*

---

1 Bailey, S. [louisamayalcottismypassion]. (2014, June 17). *I Will Remember You (for Louisa and Lizzie)* [Video file]. Retrieved from https://www.youtube.com/watch?v=V50w2J8qZXk

I am a lifelong New Englander, fortunate to have lived less than an hour away from the Alcott homestead/museum in Concord, Massachusetts. The product of a mixed marriage (my father is Roman Catholic and my mother is Unitarian), my inner life was fed both by my father's church and my mother's appreciation for nature. As a family we often went out on walks, the high point being the visit to Mount Auburn Cemetery in Cambridge every Mother's Day to take in the flora and view the spring migration of birds. It's no wonder that when I first learned of Transcendentalism that it all felt familiar.

I encountered Louisa May Alcott for the first time through a book given to me by my Aunt Petty. It was a children's biography called *The Story of Louisa May Alcott* by Joan Howard. Before that book, I hadn't paid much attention. My second grade teacher had assigned an abridged version of *Little Women* to read but I never finished it. I was, however, drawn to the chapters focused on Beth; I ended up reading "The Valley of the Shadow" multiple times. Attracted to Beth's goodness, I have always associated her name with beauty. But it was Joan Howard's book, with the wonderful illustrations by Flora Smith, that drew me into Louisa May Alcott's amazing story.

**Meeting Louisa**

Upon opening Howard's book I met 'Louy.' This was how Louisa's family addressed her because they knew she wished to have a more boyish name. She was an all-out tomboy, so bold and creative; I became lost within her world. She wrote and produced plays with her sisters just like I did with the neighbors. I mimicked her writing in apple trees by climbing into our little crabapple tree, pencil and pad in hand. I felt her appreciation for having a room of her own, a space to be alone, think and create. I had trouble fitting in, as did she. And at last I had found a friend with a temper as fierce as mine.

I began to write poetry and create little books, bound and with illustrations. I helped start a neighborhood newspaper just as Louisa had created "The Olive Leaf" to entertain her family. I read that book given to me by my aunt so many times that I nearly wore it out. It was the beginning of my on-again, off-again secret passion with Louisa May Alcott's life.

**Growing up with Louisa**

My interests turned towards music after discovering the guitar at age fifteen; writing poetry morphed into songwriting. While dreaming of a career as a professional singer/songwriter, I discovered Louisa the artist through the reading of my first adult biography on Alcott, Martha Saxton's provocative *Louisa May Alcott: A Modern Biography*. The cover, featuring the now-famous daguerreotype of Louisa in her mid-twenties, along with lurid drawings of Victorian women with men, drew me in like a magnet. I was struck by Louisa's dark beauty and haunted expression. Within those pages I found someone who, like me, was driven to create. I encountered my 'friend's' difficulty with her smoking temper that often expressed itself in depression; this too was my experience. I learned what it meant to have an artistic temperament (something I was told I had by my art teacher) and how it expressed itself sometimes in manic episodes of creativity. While I gave into my episodes, I found it hard to live with what I called my 'beast,' that force of creativity which would transform me into someone no one would want to be around. Alcott embraced her beast within, diving into her vortex, unafraid. Just as Louisa had lost herself in her writing, I was doing the same with music, writing songs and recording into the night. Louisa was no longer just a friend with interests like mine; she became my companion for the artistic journey.

That encounter with a grown-up Louisa grew into a pattern of reading a biography during the autumn season and then visiting Orchard House on pilgrimage. Still keeping my passion mostly to myself, I read books by Madeleine B. Stern, Katharine Anthony and Madelon Bedell. As I learned more about the Alcotts I became fascinated with all the family members, most especially Elizabeth, who died young like Beth and seemed mysterious. Yet for some unknown reason I never cracked open a book *by* Louisa. *Little Women* remained unread.

**Filling an empty space**

It was not until I lost my mother in my early fifties that this periodic interest became a full-time passion. *Hospital Sketches*, Alcott's faintly disguised fictional account of her service as a Civil War nurse, would be the first of her books to capture my attention, but not until I dove into a new account of Alcott's life.

My father's death in 2003 sparked the beginning of my mother's slow descent into illness, despair and dementia. In the spring of 2010, she succumbed. My siblings and I had devoted ourselves to her care and we were spent. I could not cry; I was numb, feeling only relief that her suffering was over. The music to which I had devoted nearly forty years of my life had died within me with the passing of my parents. My life was empty, waiting for the next chapter.

I had always thought my interest in Louisa was a secret but apparently someone was paying attention. During the last year of my mother's life my husband had bought two new books on Alcott for me: a biography and a novel. It was six months before I could look at them, but when the time came, I was grateful beyond words for his thoughtfulness.

In late April of 2010 I began reading *The Lost Summer of Louisa May Alcott* by Kelly O'Connor McNees. It was the perfect springtime book, a fictional account of a mid-twenties Louisa in Walpole, New Hampshire, and her romance with a handsome store clerk, Joseph Singer. As Alcott had remained single throughout her life, many friends and acquaintances speculated on whether or not she had been involved in a serious romance (there were mentions of her Polish 'boy' Ladislas Wisniewski, whom she credited along with Alf Whitman as the inspiration for Laurie in *Little Women;* she and Laddie spent a whirlwind fourteen days together in Paris). *Lost Summer* drew me back into a world that I had not visited in a long time. I had missed my 'friend' more than I knew.

While reading *Lost Summer*, my husband alerted me to a documentary airing on PBS on Louisa May Alcott; the first of its kind, it was titled *Louisa May Alcott: The Woman Behind Little Women*. It was exciting seeing Alcott portrayed on the small screen. This led to the reading of the accompanying biography by Harriet Reisen, the second of the two books that my husband had given me. It proved to be a game changer. I learned many new facts about Louisa's life from Reisen's lively account. But more importantly, it was her knowledge of and passion for the author's canon that finally drove me to read Alcott's works. Thus I began with *Hospital Sketches,* inspired by

Reisen's description of Louisa's brief service as a Civil War nurse.

**Louisa as grief counselor**

*Hospital Sketches* was the right book at the right time. My 'friend' not only seemed to understand my artistic journey but also my grief and my faith. Reisen's book revealed that Louisa had nursed her dying sister and although Louisa's sorrow was profound after Lizzie's death, she admitted in her journal that "I don't miss her as I expected to do, for she seems nearer and dearer than before; and I am glad to know she is safe from pain and age in some world where her innocent soul must be happy."[2] Her thoughts were much like my own after the numbness had begun to melt away. Like her I believed in an afterlife, convinced that my mother was in a better place.

Louisa's care for Lizzie qualified her to serve as a Civil War nurse. She became intimately involved with her patients, calling them "my boys" and writing about them in the letters home that were to become *Hospital Sketches*. In the fourth chapter, "A Night," she described a particular soldier for whom she had grown fond, a Virginia blacksmith by the name of John Suhre. He was a big man: strong, handsome, and yet with many of the virtues of her departed sister. Louisa, calling herself "Nurse Tribulation Periwinkle" in the book, held his hand as his life's breath departed, helping him to bear the pain. John Suhre became a precursor to Beth March in *Little Women*.

2 Alcott, L. M. (1890). *Louisa May Alcott: Her Life, Letters and Journals* (E. D. Cheney, Ed.). Boston: Roberts Brothers, p. 98.

Reisen pointed out how Louisa's writing had evolved from fantasy and potboilers to real life. In the midst of loss, grief and war, she discovered her true voice. That voice in turn spoke to a public hungry for anything coming from the war front. Through Nurse Tribulation Periwinkle, readers could virtually experience life in an army hospital, drawing them closer to their loved ones far away from home. Touched with humor and pathos, the urgent realism of Louisa's writing sprinkled with her eternal optimism consoled and inspired readers from her time, launching her career as a popular author. Those words continue to inspire and console today.

It was the beginning of an interest in my favorite author's inner life. In *Hospital Sketches*, Louisa's beliefs spoke to me, especially when it came to suffering and death. She held these as sacred, redemptive to the dying while illuminating to the living. I could relate to that, hold on to it, and from it draw consolation and understanding.

I needed that consolation. I had trouble remembering what my mother had been like when she was healthy: this was the woman whose zest for life, endless curiosity, love of nature, fierce devotion to her family and endearing thoughtfulness had shaped and inspired me. She had been my confidante and best friend and now she appeared gone from my memory.

But she left something behind that helped me to reconnect with her: copies of *Little Women, Aunt Jo's Scrap-Bag* and *An Old-Fashioned Girl*, each marked with her personal bookplate. In thumbing through those pages I felt as though I was sitting alongside my mother when she had been young and vital, reading along with her. Tears streamed down my face as I read yet again "The

Valley of the Shadow" from her copy of *Little Women*. It was the first time that I had been able to cry.

**No longer alone in my passion**

In past years it would have been enough to read these books and visit Orchard House. Not this time. Now I had a strong urge to meet with other Alcott fans and talk with them about Louisa's life and works, to learn from them and to share experiences. Harriet Reisen and I had been communicating by email after I sent her a comment about her book. Most times I shy away from the phone, but caught up in my desire, I asked if we could talk, as she lived nearby. For an hour Ms. Reisen listened to a stranger pour out her heart about her love of Louisa May Alcott. To this day I am grateful for her generosity and graciousness.

That conversation stoked the fire. I began searching for websites where the conversation could continue. After finding static sites that gave information but offered no community, I decided to build my own. Struggling through a steep learning curve with WordPress, I created *Louisa May Alcott is My Passion* in August of 2010. The response was immediate. My dream of building a community of Alcott enthusiasts, from fan and student to educator and scholar, had begun and has since surpassed every expectation.

**Reading *Little Women* at last**

At age 54 I settled down to read *Little Women* in full for the first time. As I pored over it I posted on the blog, enjoying the back and forth with my readers. Yet the book did not resonate as I expected it would; I was missing what others could plainly see. I longed to know the mind of typical readers from the post-Civil War era so that I could better understand their guttural reaction to *Little Women.* My thoughts about the story contradicted those of the majority of readers. To begin with, I was not particularly fond of Jo March. I saw her as a bit of a troublemaker, going out of her way to be contrary. Her reaction to Meg's engagement and subsequent marriage seemed quite odd (until I read the author's own words in her journal). Unlike most, I thought Professor Bhaer was the better fit for Jo. I surprised myself by proclaiming Amy as my favorite March sister, impressed at her maturation from a selfish, petted child to a gracious and generous young lady.

Beth remained unchanged in my mind. I still cried when she died, more so because I had come to know her kind heart and courage in the face of suffering (especially when she took the sick Hummel baby into her lap, only to have it die). Her encounter with Mr. Laurence after he gave her the piano was the most touching scene in the book. She was as beautiful to me as ever.

I believe that my extensive knowledge of the author placed me at a disadvantage for appreciating this book, particularly when it came to Jo March. Most Alcott fans are introduced to Louisa by her stories (especially *Little Women*) whereas I had first been introduced to her life. The end result was Jo appearing as a mere shadow of the real woman.

It took a second reading for the power of *Little Women* to sink in. Jo did turn out to be the reason for my growing appreciation but not because she was a writer. Rather, it was because of Alcott's nuanced description of Jo's growth into womanhood, molded through her journey of grief after Beth's passing. Those years of living with my own had demonstrated the creative power of grief in transforming a person. That change can be for good or for naught. The process is inevitable; we only have to choose how that force works within us.

Jo allowed grief to take her in a positive direction, opening up to love outside of the immediate family circle. Meg noted that her sister was like a chestnut burr, "prickly outside, but silky-soft within, and a sweet kernel, if one can only get at it." She felt certain the love of a man would enter into her sister's heart, causing that burr to fall away.[3] Such change was not without significant struggle. Having taken Beth's exhortation quite literally to "be everything to father and mother," Jo renounced her writing ambition (and thus her identity), trying in vain to become her sister.[4] She soon learned this was not possible; she had to find the way that best suited her disposition. Turning to her parents for counsel, Jo resumed the course of her life by embracing what she had previously set aside. It would take many years on a long and crooked path to achieve her dream. In the course of her life, other unexpected dreams would be realized (including marriage to Professor Bhaer and motherhood). In the end she became everything to her parents by being herself.

**Returning to my roots**

Like Jo, I allowed grief to transform me. It gently carried me back to my lifelong childhood 'friend.' Starting up the blog not only rekindled an interest in the writing

3 Alcott, L.M. (2013). *Little Women: An Annotated Edition* (D. Shealy, ed.) Cambridge, MA: Belknap Press of Harvard Univ. Press, p. 515.

4 *Ibid*, p. 533.

I had abandoned years before, it also created a hunger for knowledge of the Alcotts that grew into an obsession. Soon I began taking trips to the Concord Library's Special Collections to see pages in Louisa's hand from *Little Women*. I copied a touching letter that Louisa had written to her cousin Eliza Wells about the death of Lizzie. I spent hours squinting at a microfiche reader, poring over letters from different family members. A year after the blog began, I made the first of many trips to Harvard University's Houghton Library to read Lizzie's childhood diary and delve more into the family letters. As I saw the ink and touched the paper, icons turned into long lost relatives. Reading Lizzie's words in particular created a desire to tell her life's story. With so little written by her or about her by the family (with the exception of her last illness), there did not seem to be much to go on. What could I possibly discover and reveal that had eluded every Alcott biographer? It was a mystery I intended to solve. After several years of research, having amassed hundreds of photographs of family letters and journals (and a bibliography a mile long), I am now ready to begin.

It is true that what goes around comes around: Beth March had been my favorite as a child; now in my later years I am led back to her as I work to tell the story of Elizabeth Alcott's life. My dear 'friend' Louisa continues to guide me.

It is hard to know just how far this passion for Louisa May Alcott will go but it has certainly yielded a multitude of blessings. Writing the blog led to the authoring of two books, one a spiritual memoir (*River of Grace: Creative Passages Through Difficult Times*, Ave Maria Press) and the other, a devotional pairing Bible verses with sections from Louisa's stories (*Louisa May Alcott: Illuminated by*

*The Message*, ACTA Publications). I call many Alcott fans, aficionados, educators and scholars 'friends' and enjoy gathering with them every summer at Orchard House for their Summer Conversational Series. Recently I was able to collaborate with one such friend in revealing the discovery of previously unpublished photographs of Anna Alcott Pratt and her husband John. And the blog continues to reach out to Alcott lovers, building the community.

There is no doubt: Louisa May Alcott will always be my passion.

## About the Author

***Susan Bailey*** is the webmaster for the blog *Louisa May Alcott is My Passion*. She has authored two books, *Louisa May Alcott: Illuminated by The Message* (ACTA Publications) and *River of Grace: Creative Passages Through Difficult Times* (Ave Maria Press). Susan is currently working on a biography of Elizabeth Sewall Alcott. She is an active member of the Louisa May Alcott Society, Louisa May Alcott's Orchard House and the Fruitlands Museum.

# Pilgrim's Regress

*by Deborah Davis Schlacks*

ᔓ

On a Monday in April, several years ago, my daughter Laura and I visited Orchard House, home of Louisa May Alcott and her family. I remember a brown frame house. I remember the walls of May Alcott's room, covered with May's drawings. That room is vivid in my memory. Most of all, I remember a drawing of a goddess in advance of a chariot in which sat a man, leading him and a company of other goddesses and a cupid onward in triumph, a powerful visual message on a bedroom wall.

But I remember nothing else about the house, even though by all rights I should remember it much better. I've tried to remember more, but the memories will not come. There is a reason for the amnesia: something that happened right after our visit that occupies the crevices in my brain where other Orchard House images ought to be.

"April is the cruelest month," I'd thought, almost as a reflex, as I arrived in Boston the previous Friday. Back at my home in northern Wisconsin, I often quoted this line from Eliot when the snow fell in April even though it should have been spring. But here, on the precipice of a pleasant, long Patriot Day weekend, with spring weather aplenty in Boston, the quote seemed like just a joke.

Laura met me at the Boston airport. We were headed for a weekend in New Hampshire, where I (an English professor) was to attend a conference. Then we'd be back on Sunday evening and would spend Monday—Patriot Day itself—sightseeing.

For months, we'd been planning what to do with our time on Monday. The Boston Marathon? Not on your life. It was sure to be a mob scene at the finish line, something my claustrophobic constitution did not relish. What, instead, about the Patriot Day observance in Concord, we'd mused. As a Southerner who'd lived for the past 20 years in the upper Midwest, I'd never experienced Patriot Day before. And what about following up with visits to Walden Pond and Orchard House?

Once we'd thought of those possibilities, the die was immediately cast. We'd do all three. I was particularly anxious to tour Orchard House. An avid fan of Louisa May Alcott for many years, I'd read *Little Women* literally dozens of times as a girl and now, decades later, still remembered every jot and tittle of it: Jo wanting to go off to war to be a nurse, Jo cutting off her hair to sell to finance her mother's trip to be with her ailing father, Jo taking care of her dying sister Beth, Jo becoming a writer—writing, among other things, a poem about her dead sister that had made me cry upon every single reading. I had also long been fascinated by Louisa May Alcott herself. I'd read of her short-lived career as a Civil War nurse, her family's involvement in the Underground Railroad, and much more.

So we went to Orchard House the afternoon of Patriot Day, after watching the Revolutionary War reenactment at the Patriot Day commemoration, after dipping our hands into Walden Pond.

Coming back to our hotel room in Concord after the visit to Orchard House, I switched on the TV, and we encountered pandemonium. It was the Marathon bombing. It had just happened. The story unfolded more and more for the rest of the afternoon, as we watched the coverage and realized the extent of the disaster. People were dead and gravely injured, and no one knew yet at whose hands.

By and by, Monday evening loomed. I had to take my daughter back to her dorm, as she would have classes the next day, and I'd be leaving for home early in the morning so I could teach a class Tuesday afternoon. At least I hoped I could get home on schedule. Shortly after the bombing, the airport had been shut down, for fear the bombers would try to escape town by plane. And as we drove that evening back to BC, the traffic was bumper-to-bumper, even worse than usual for Boston, and I feared all the more how hard it might be the next day to make the trip back to Wisconsin.

Surprisingly, however, things went smoothly at first the next day. I drove to the airport in the dark, the streets almost deserted now. I turned in my rental car, found my way through airport security very much as usual, and eventually found myself on the plane, which, remarkably, was scheduled for an on-time departure.

Soon enough as I drifted off to sleep, I realized someone was standing beside my aisle seat. I looked up. A man who appeared to be Middle Eastern was asking me to get up and let him in: his was the middle seat. As I complied, he said something in what sounded like Arabic to another man who was passing him in the aisle.

They were apparently together. When he could get by, his companion went back a couple of rows to his own seat.

Minutes later, a sky marshal entered the plane, approaching our row. He asked the Middle Eastern-looking man beside me and then his companion to get off the plane. I started to sense tension among the passengers: first one, and then another, and then another head turned as folks seemed to be trying to see and hear what was going on in our row and in the row where the second man was sitting. People's expressions were tense.

More minutes passed. Then a flight attendant came to my row. "It looks like they're going to let them back on," she said worriedly to me and the window-seat man. "But," she continued, "when they're back, be vigilant, and if you notice *anything*, let us know *immediately*." And again, heads turned and expressions tensed at her words.

This entire situation was getting out of hand, I said to myself. Was there any real danger with these particular men? If so, I thought, just don't bring them back on. If not, don't foment panic and worry like this. In the meantime, I realized with the extra time we were spending waiting for the men to be questioned, I was going to miss my connection in Chicago—a small matter in the scheme of things, of course.

A few minutes later, the two men re-boarded and took their seats. The window-seat man asked the man who sat in the middle seat where he was heading. Disneyland, he said.

The plane started taxiing. The middle seat man turned his head and said something in Arabic (as I suppose it was) to his companion. Heads whipped around. The taxiing continued. Then the other man got up and went to the restroom in the back of the plane. Heads whipped around again. This time, a flight attendant rushed from the front to the back of the plane.

Heads whipped around one more time. I have to confess: mine did, too, this time. Mine did, too.

"We're going back to the gate," said the captain over the speaker moments later. "Then everyone has to get off the plane so we can sweep it."

Back at the gate, while exiting the plane, I heard a little boy tell his mother, "Tell them they need to sweep the toilet. He might have put something in there."

"That's a good idea," said the mother. "Did you hear what he just said?" she said in a proud voice to the man beside her, as if her son were a prodigy for having thought of it. "They need to sweep inside the toilet. They might not think of that."

And I heard someone else say, "Everything would have been all right if only they hadn't done what they'd done." Done what they'd done? Talked in their native language to each other? Gone to the restroom? I thought these things but said nothing. Why couldn't I have said something that would at least have let these two men know that not everyone on that plane assumed they must be up to no good?

Back in the airport, chaos reigned as folks arranged for different flights since many had missed their connections or else didn't want to go back onto that plane regardless of the fate of their connections. As I stood in line, I noticed the two Middle Eastern-looking men talking to an agent at another desk. She was handing them new boarding passes.

Then the next day (or was it the one after?) came the news that the two bombers had been identified. They had remained in Boston the whole time in the aftermath.

And they were not Middle Eastern. The men on our plane were not the right men. They were just men wanting to get to Disneyland.

So it is that I do not remember Orchard House very well. Instead I remember the bombing that had occurred just 30 miles away from me and my daughter: the loss of life, the loss of limbs, along with the personal horror of thinking that my daughter and I had considered going to the marathon, and the personal horror of learning later that the bombers had considered bombing the Patriot Day observance that we had in fact attended that fateful Monday morning. I remember, most especially, in vast detail, the abortive plane ride the morning after. I remember the little boy telling his mother to remind the crew to sweep the toilet. I remember heads whipping round in fear—in the end, mine included. I remember all that and more about that Tuesday morning.

And I feel complicit. I was caught up in an incident of racial profiling. But to use the passive voice—"was caught up"—does not feel quite honest. It would be easy to be satisfied that internally, wordlessly, I objected to what was happening, to other people's all-too-ready assumption that these two men were to be feared. It would also be easy to justify my having also become fearful by saying that I kept wondering if the officials—the marshal, the flight attendant, the captain—knew something neither I nor my fellow passengers could have known about the two men, that they had a real, concrete reason to suspect those particular individuals. But if that had been the case, the marshal wouldn't have let them back on the plane, now would he? And it would be easy, too, to reason that I couldn't have done anything about what was happening anyway, and that is probably the case. I could not have stopped it. But to have stayed silent? It is the not-having-spoken-up that I am haunted by.

Louisa May Alcott's home served as a station on the Underground Railroad before the war. Then, during the Civil War, Louisa May Alcott served briefly as a nurse. She became very ill and had to quit, but I have no doubt she would have pressed onward in this duty if she could have. As it was, she suffered for the rest of her life from complications of the mercury-based treatment she received for her illness contracted in the wartime hospital. In short, she was a woman of grit, courage, and resolve, someone not afraid to take risks, someone who stood up for what she believed in.

Further, Louisa May Alcott had a voice that she used: she was a writer. She wrote of her nursing experiences in *Hospital Sketches.* She created Jo March, who echoes Louisa's own background in significant ways, with Jo's desire to be a nurse in wartime, nursing of a sick sister, and writing efforts. I am reminded of Martin Luther King Jr., who in one of his most famous pronouncements said, "In the end, we will remember not the words of our enemies, but the silence of our friends." Words do have power. Louisa May Alcott knew that. Silence, on the other hand, can speak its own kind of volumes. King knew that.

I wonder what Louisa would have done in my shoes. It is hard to transport her into the 21st century and to know what she would have made of the situation in which I found myself. Would she have spoken up then and there? I do not know. But I do firmly believe that even if she had not, she would have found a way to write about it, letting the words in a story or an essay make the point. That is, after all, a way of not remaining silent. And so, I write here about that cruel April. It is all I can do, since I cannot go back in time. Like May's drawings at Orchard House, the message is, I hope, now on the wall.

## About the Author

***Deborah Davis Schlacks*** is Professor Emerita of English at the University of Wisconsin-Superior. She retired from the university in May 2018 after a 22-year career there teaching writing and literature. Before UW-Superior, she taught for 10 years at the University of Nevada-Las Vegas. A native of the small town of Howe, Texas, she received a PhD in English in 1986 from Texas Woman's University in Denton. Her literary specialty is American literature. She has published scholarly works on F. Scott Fitzgerald and has done conference presentations on such authors as Fitzgerald, Hemingway, and Louisa May Alcott. She first read *Little Women* as a third grader and proceeded to re-read the book dozens and dozens of times. As a girl, she aspired to have four daughters named Meg, Jo, Beth, and Amy. She and her husband, Eric, really do have two daughters named Beth and Laura, and they also have a son-in-law named Tim, a dog named Scout, and a cat named Delilah. They live on Amnicon Lake in far-northern Wisconsin, near a town called Superior, which is on the tip of Lake Superior.

# Why Jo Says No (and Why We Care)

*by Trix Wilkins*

ᔓ

The first time I read *Little Women*, I wasn't too surprised Jo said no.

I was, however, shocked when I reached the end of *Good Wives* and found that no still standing. For the last twenty odd years I've been wondering about Jo and Laurie and discovering I'm not alone.

Why did Jo say no? Why did she keep saying no? And why do we care so much that she did?

**Why Jo says no the first time**

Jo and Laurie's friendship starts off like a fairy tale—dances and laughter in the hallway on New Year's Eve, a bold winter visit to comfort the ill boy living in the "mansion of bliss" next door, a mutual love of books and music. Laurie seems slated to be the match for *Little Women's* fiery Jo.

Then he goes to college—and spends his money on clothes, flirts with other women, and makes as little of his studies as possible. The text doesn't say why. He simply becomes a dandy until Jo tells him to shape up. To his credit, he then digs in and graduates with honors.

Still, it's not enough. To his dismay, she has other reasons to say no.

*Marmee said they didn't suit*

Who can say no to Marmee—the conscience of the family, whose approval all the girls seek? When Jo realizes that Laurie is eyeing her for his wife, she makes plans to "go away for a time." Marmee agrees with this idea, telling Jo that she and Laurie don't suit each other for marriage. Thus, when Laurie proposes, Jo declines: *Marmee says we won't work out—so no.*

*She thought Beth was in love with Laurie*

When I think of my own sister, I often ask myself whether I'm loving her as well as Jo loves Beth. Just as Laurie's affection for Jo is taking flight, Jo catches Beth looking at Laurie and imagines Beth is in love with him. Nothing could persuade Jo to hurt her by becoming the wife of the man Beth loves. Again, the answer must be no.

*She didn't think she was good enough for him*

She's clear about this in her refusal—she tells him she thinks him "a great deal too good" for her, if she said yes he'd resent her for being an antisocial writer, and he'll inevitably long for a "fine mistress" for his stately home. Her high view of him is telling in the closing chapter—Jo says that when her school opens she'll point to Laurie and say, "Here's the sort of man you want to be!"

*Marriage was not Plan A*

When Jo talks about her castle in the air, there's no master in it. She wants to be a rich and famous author. At the time Laurie proposes, she's just had a taste of literary success. She's eager to get out in the world, to write new things, see new things. Saying yes to marriage meant yes to becoming a wife (and possibly having children)—with less freedom and time for Plan A.

*Being Laurie's wife was a job she didn't want*

Jo expects Laurie will follow in his grandfather's footsteps. This isn't a life she'd sit comfortably in—she is not generally sociable and doesn't care for others' opinions. As an India merchant, Laurie would be absent for weeks, perhaps months—meanwhile, Jo's to carry on with … calls. Were she to be his wife, Jo would feel obliged to do things she detests for his sake.

*It was bad timing …*

Laurie's just graduated. He's about to do the Grand Tour. Why not whisk Jo away to Europe? This might have been a good idea, were there family-planning options and if Laurie actually had a career idea (if he weren't resisting his grandfather's take-over-the-family-business-after-college deal, for example, or had a back-up plan). He's not ready to be a husband and father—and so Jo says no.

*There's already Something about the Professor*

While she's saying no, Jo reveals she has an incredible amount of respect for Friedrich Bhaer. Laurie has Jo's friendship, but Friedrich has Jo's esteem. For her to accept the proposal of one man while esteeming another *more* would have been disastrous. Did Jo think of this at the time? If she did, she didn't say so, but for my part I'm glad she said no with such a dynamic in play.

## Why Jo keeps saying no

Confession: I read *Pride and Prejudice* before I read *Good Wives.* So when Laurie proposes and Jo initially says no, guess what I think I see coming? Laurie saves the sister, pulls up his boots, and gets the girl.

Why does this not happen? Why does Jo keep saying no?

### *Not enough has changed*

Even with the passage of time, Laurie still hasn't worked out what to do with his life when he asks Jo a second time. In fact, he's gone back to what he was doing in his college days—being a dandy, flirting, throwing away talent and money—just on a different continent.

### *It was still bad timing …*

Nobody told Amy that Jo rejected Laurie. So there's no reason for Amy to omit from her letters home the fact that she and Laurie are having a grand time in Europe (or to mention what he has—or has not—been doing there). Meanwhile, Jo's reading letters about Laurie's wastefulness and frivolity while Beth is wasting away in her arms. Again—bad timing.

## Why we care so much

One hundred fifty years the publication of *Little Women*, Jo's rejection of Laurie still bothers a lot of people.

It still bothers me.

Why? Why do we care so much about this particular plot point? Why does it raise so much ire for so many that Jo rejected Laurie? (And that he gave up?)

*It really is personal—to us*

The reason we care might not be that complicated. It might be personal, perhaps as straightforward as, "Well, I married my best friend and I'm happy!" Or maybe we trusted someone who gave us advice that went awry, and we read of Jo listening to Marmee unquestioningly and we shake the book: "Don't do it! Test everything! Argh!"

*On principle, the reason "Marmee said so" doesn't fly*

There's nothing wrong with testing the idea of a person one trusts. If they're wrong, we can correct them; if not, we can be convinced. We care about Jo's saying no because of what readers learn about handling advice and information even from trusted sources. Are we boldly learning to test ideas for truth? Or are we learning to develop unhealthy dependence on the judgment of others?

*If there are diamonds to be found, we want to see digging*

When Jo meets Laurie, he doesn't see her as a 'diamond in the rough'—he sees her *as a diamond.* He sees the beauty of her character. We want to see him hold on to his conviction that she is worthy of persistent pursuit. That's why when he doesn't—and he fritters away his talent and money before marrying someone else—it's such a bitter pill to swallow.

*The loss of what might have been*

It's not just about the romance that might have been—it's also about the man Laurie might have become. Laurie might have set up the school with Jo (we see in the sequels how much he enjoys being involved in the school). He might have written books and music (he loved both). Instead, he responds badly to the first no, and the no stays a no. And we lament what might have been.

*We want to reward loyalty*

We want the one who has been there the whole time to get the girl. It seems just. We long for Laurie to win Jo for the sheer reason that he has loved her for so long, and loved her despite the quarrels, the differences, the heartaches.

*We want the girl who doesn't chase the boy to get the boy*

Jo doesn't pursue Laurie and that's precisely why we want her to have him. We want to see the girl who doesn't chase the boy get the boy—to be loved by him no matter the setbacks. (And we want our daughters to grow up with the idea that it's a good thing *not* to chase a boy.)

*We like to see people work through the hard stuff*

It's not that we love a good fight (well, maybe sometimes), but we are thrilled when we're able to say to ourselves, "That was hard. But we sorted it out. We made it work." There's a sense of accomplishment and immense satisfaction in overcoming challenges. With Jo and Laurie, we were deprived of that—and it's hard not to feel dull disappointment.

*It feels like a smackdown of our worldview*

Jo's choice challenges values we may have come to hold tightly: the ideas of resisting norms (Jo's marriage to the professor conforms to what is expected of her—marriage to a man within her social status), of setting goals and achieving them (Jo abandons writing), and of critically thinking (Jo unquestioningly follows Marmee's advice). When our worldview is challenged, the first reaction is often emotional (and unpleasant).

*Economics is not always fun, but it's necessary*

Having choices takes money (consider: Jo might have written books if she'd married Laurie). Jo's saying no feels like a refusal to admit this reality. Did Louisa write this into *Little Women* as a critique of her father's view of money, to incite outrage by showing that those who don't hold such a view can still suffer by the neglect of those who do? If she did, she definitely stirred that pot.

*We long for the exceptional*

It's easy to find a relationship between a rich, handsome guy and a charming, beautiful girl (in books as well as life). However, not all of us want to find the everyday in a book—we want to see the exception. For many readers, Theodore Laurence patiently and persistently courting Jo March until she came to love him would have been the exceptional choice.

*It really is personal—to Louisa May Alcott*

When I first read of how hard Louisa's life had been, and how she had given up her romance with Ladislas 'Laddie' Wisniewski, I cried. The account of this time is scratched out in her diary, a note left in the margins: "Couldn't be." Of their parting, Louisa wrote, "I drew down his tall head and kissed him tenderly, feeling that in this world there were no more meetings for us."

Why this was is lost to history. The best guess I have read espoused is that Louisa denied herself so she could work to provide for her family. After discovering this, I felt the full force of why Jo had to say no and cried some more (and wrote my book, *The Courtship of Jo March*).

When Louisa first wrote *Little Women*, she didn't expect it to succeed. She wasn't expecting public scrutiny of her private life. She could write about Jo and Laurie having a wonderful friendship and hint at a possible romance because she didn't expect to write what came next.

Then *Little Women* sold the world over, and what a bind Louisa found herself in.

She couldn't write such a romance in good conscience even if she wanted to explore what it *could be*. Now there were real consequences involved. The real Laurie was alive and had a real future. As popular as such an ending between Jo and Laurie might have been, I suspect Louisa didn't allow herself to play it out on paper for Laddie's sake. The real Jo truly cared for the real Laurie.

That's why we care. That's why we feel Jo's refusal bitterly, personally.

Because it *was* personal. Jo's final no is real. It is what Louisa actually said to a chance at love.

*It's at the heart of why Little Women still matters*

As much as it breaks hearts, Jo's no is a huge part of why *Little Women* resonates and has done so for the last century and a half. "There is truth in it," Jo's mother tells her. The truth will often be hard to swallow, but we will always care for it to be told. We will always need it to be told.

And for those of us who still wonder, we can always imagine what might have been.

## About the Author

***Trix Wilkins*** isn't a *Little Women* scholar, academic, or PhD. She just really enjoys reading the novel (especially the bits about Jo and Laurie) and writing about it on her blog *Much Ado about Little Women*. And, because she married her best friend and wishes Jo had done the same, she wrote *The Courtship of Jo March*.

# Super Marmee

*by Adrienne Quintana*

ꕥ

My mom first introduced me to *Little Women* when I was twelve years old. 1988. Dad's career as an oil landscape artist was beginning to take off. My parents decided to pull us out of public school so we could travel with them to art shows around the country.

Homeschooling was a gutsy move at the time. People weren't really doing it back then unless they lived on a remote compound in northern Idaho or Texas. But my mom was passionate. She was convinced that she was ready to take our education into her own hands.

Heading into uncharted waters, Mom tested out different methods, schedules, and curriculums, but one thing remained consistent over the years: Mom read to us. She chose a variety of books, most often classic children's literature, and we gathered around her worn leather chair in our tiny living room or listened to her read from the back of our passenger van. We listened to her lilting voice day after day, mile after mile, page after page. *Little Women* came somewhere between *The Lion, the Witch and the Wardrobe* and *Tom Sawyer*.

But *Little Women* was different from the others. It was about my sisters and me. Like so many before and after us, we saw ourselves in the characters Alcott had created. Beautiful, quiet Yvette was a mixture of Meg and Beth, Shalece was the artistically talented Amy, and I, of course, was Jo. We were still young, but we saw a glimpse of our own futures as we watched the March girls grow up.

Something we failed to recognize as Mom's sleepy voice read just one more chapter before bed, was that there was another Alcott character with whom we would each eventually connect. A character almost invisible to us as young girls. Someone we would all become.

Marmee.

Just like my own mom, Marmee disappears into the background of Alcott's story. It isn't about her. She isn't really a main character. She's there, but her role is to take care of things. She takes care of the household. She takes care of the neighbors. She takes care of the sick and wounded.

The story isn't about her, and yet we get a sense of how extraordinary Marmee is. From the Christmas breakfast given to the Hummels to the very last line in the book, Marmee's philosophies, values, and beliefs are sprinkled on almost every page. Through her example, both words and deeds, Marmee teaches her little women how to find true happiness.

My mom did the same for me. Just like Marmee, she married for love and found herself in humble circumstances. Instead of complaining about what she lacked, my mom was optimistic and grateful. She went looking for people who were less fortunate than us, and she served them and shared what little we had with them.

Like the virtuous woman described in Proverbs 31, my mom opened her "mouth with wisdom; and in her tongue [was] the law of kindness." No matter how angry I was with someone in a given situation, she always tried to help me see the good in the other person. None of my siblings ever tried to burn my manuscript, but if they had, I'm sure my mom would have encouraged me not to "let the sun go down upon [my] anger." Like Marmee, she taught me to forgive and move on.

But my mom and Marmee weren't only about service and kindness. They had strong political opinions and they weren't afraid to express them openly. They had ideas about how to make the world a better place, and they were willing to execute them, even if it meant sacrifice. Even if it meant standing alone. They were revolutionaries.

I don't remember where or when my mom finished reading *Little Women* to us, but I do remember watching the Winona Ryder movie version with my sisters the year I graduated from high school. Our original character picks still stood, and within a few years proved accurate. Quiet Yvette married young and focused on home and family. Shalece spent time in Italy and became an artist. I continued to write, and eventually published. Just like Meg, Jo, Beth, and Amy, our personalities, talents, and interests led us down very different paths, but those paths all ended up in the same place.

As individual and unique as each of Alcott's little women are, eventually, the story stops being about them and they become Marmee.

## About the Author

***Adrienne Quintana*** is the author of *Eruption* and *Reclamation*, as well as several children's books. When she isn't writing, Adrienne enjoys running, hiking, and matchmaking. (Are you single? She probably knows someone perfect for you.) She lives in Arizona with her husband and four children, who give her love, support, and plenty of good material for Instagram.

# Little Rivals

*by Rachel Roberts*

ꝏ

*"I detest rude, unlady-like girls!"*
*"I hate affected, niminy-piminy chits."*

—"Playing Pilgrims," *Little Women*

Foils in the most contentious March relationship, are tomboy Jo and precocious Amy more alike than they first seem? Like them, growing up I longed to travel, be creative and discover some elusive calling and, to my detriment, viewed peers who had this ambition with some hostility. Of course, I felt instant connection to Jo. Her clumsiness, angst and earnestness made her relatable, yet she was vivid and courageous. While Meg and Beth faded into the background, Amy stood out as an antagonist. However, Jo and Amy clash—not because of their differences, but because they are competing for the same limited opportunities.

From the outset their relationship lacks the supportive element of other sisterly connections. Adolescents Meg and Jo sustain one another through trials of service; Meg mentors Amy in beauty and propriety; Jo and Beth have rejected society (albeit for different reasons) with gentle Beth inspiring Jo to moderate herself.

The first spat comes in "Jo Meets Apollyon" with the catalyst of the girls vying for Laurie's attention. A lively boy is likely to cause friction when all there is to do is knit army socks and reflect on your shortcomings. The Laurence Boy has had a hard time; his parents died, his schoolmates bullied him, his grandfather is remote, his tutor is boring. Naturally, this slightly girlish boy finds a perfect pal in a boyish girl.

Jo's anger management issues are her "bosom enemy," so she takes badly to a brat burning her project of several years. Outclassed in getting her crush's attention, Amy has also reacted with rage. The outcome is unfair—Jo is wronged, but then tormented by not meeting impossible standards because her sister falls into a pond. We are given an internal view of her battle with satanic forces in her outpour to Marmee. In contrast, Amy's growth (in Volume I) is limited to sorry-you're-mad and not getting caught with pickled goods. While Meg and Beth are idealized (Meg prepares to be an exemplary wife, Beth is devoted to her parents), naughty Jo and Amy, motivated by strong self-identity, test the boundaries of parlor and schoolroom.

As they mature, Amy, socialite-on-a-budget, is determined to advance—fickle friends not bothering to turn up to her party is a major setback—while Jo struggles to find purpose, leading to feelings of alienation. They are particularly at odds in "Calls," with Jo being generally embarrassing in order to subvert Amy's efforts to win favor. The joke backfires as relatives compare notes, deciding which to take on a tour of Europe. Jo has already been passed over by Aunt March in favor of Amy's pleasant demeanor, and is found lacking once more. We resent them being compared, especially in a social media age when we claim to value authenticity over 'fakeness.' The image of Jo crying secretly, having endured Amy's departure, berating herself for not being pretty or nice enough, is relatable. Amy's letters home are the nineteenth century version of filtered Instagram posts, whereas Jo's experiences (chores and awkward conversations) feel like real life.

Both girls strive for manly careers in the arts, like Laurie, yearning for fame. The growing publishing market (of dime novels and penny dreadfuls, popular with the newly literate working class) offers a degree of financial success which ultimately comes at the cost of integrity. Shielded from family finances, Amy pursues art for art's sake. Usually forming the butt of some joke, her creativity is made out to be a delusional hobby compared to Jo's nobler ambition, reflecting that her chances are slim given that painting was the preserve of well-connected men.

Readers frequently cite the most controversial Jo-Amy development to be Laurie's failed proposal to Jo in a muddy field, followed by his growing closeness to Amy in the French Riviera, which ends in marriage. Classical literature has taught us to distrust men who switch affections between affiliated women (think Mr. Collins, *Pride and Prejudice*). Amy takes up Jo's role as Laurie's conscience, disciplining him for giving into self-pity and idleness, finally demonstrating March ethics of work and self-improvement. He influences her to renounce her aggressive pursuit of wealth. They show one another the "patience and forbearance" required in a successful marriage that Marmee saw lacking in Jo's juvenile friendship.

The newlyweds' return begins a reconciliation between the nearly estranged sisters. Laurie asserts the right of both to be loved in an almost credible assessment of coexisting marital and familial affection:

> "You both got into your right places, and I felt sure that it was well off with the old love before it was on with the new, that I could honestly share my heart between sister Jo and wife Amy, and love them dearly."

"Lord and Lady" take up residence in the Laurence home and pledge themselves to fashionable philanthropy. Jo, having endured disappointment, loss and drudgery, is still to fully come of age—cue Professor Bhaer, with whom she shares an outsider identity and a sense of social justice. As an immigrant to America, he perhaps offers hope that the restrictive society of her youth is opening.

Alcott takes care to detail the marginalized boys with whom Jo and Friedrich fill their school, devising for her unconventional heroine an ending which is simultaneously progressive and wholesome. The final scene, the school's apple-picking, is one of complete family unity. Having had the hardest path, Jo reaps the greatest harvest of self-awareness and fulfillment. Amy, rather than hindering, is fully supportive, taking care of Jo's most vulnerable ward. With no further need to compete, the bickering siblings have "got into their right places" within their family and community.

## About the Author

***Rachel Roberts*** grew up in Leeds, England. She studied English Literature at Newcastle University and lived for a time in Scotland. She currently lives in Leeds with her partner and works in housing. Rachel enjoys running and posting about cross stitch and dolls.

# As Real as Life Itself

*by K.R. Karr*

ᔓ

One of the most joyous and thrilling things about learning—and learning largely through reading books—is that it seems that the whole world is connected only by the thinnest of threads. Nearly everything I encounter seems to be a cousin or even a lover to something else that has crossed my path, and connects me to the important people in my life.

I knew *Little Women* first as a movie. I was a little woman myself when the Gillian Armstrong film arrived in theaters and of course I was drawn to it—I liked this sort of story that centered around girls and particularly sisters, one of which I was blessed and cursed with. And I know that many women and girls are disappointed that Jo does not end up with Laurie. Yet even then I thought Professor Bhaer so much more suitable in a sexy way that I only vaguely understood. I liked that he was German because the soft accent put on by Gabriel Byrne felt familiar to me. Like my German grandmother, called Oma. Come to think of it, I watched *Little Women* on video at her house a few times, too.

Watching over me watching this movie was my Oma's stone bust of Goethe, her literary love. He stood on a bookshelf with a bunch of German books, facing the TV. Oma loved him so much, in fact, that my step-grandfather referred to Goethe as his "chief rival," even inscribing this in the Goethe books he'd give her for Christmases or birthdays. How *does* one compete against the imagination and the constancy of the literary-loving heart?

This must have been difficult for him when he wanted Oma's attention, as she was deeply enamored of literature and was always off exploring her prolific and seemingly contradictory taste; on the one hand, she read tough, masculine modernists like Bertolt Brecht and D.H. Lawrence; on the other, she had a thing for girls' fiction—Nancy Drew and the works of Frances Hodgson Burnett, and she seemed familiar with *Little Women* as I watched it in her house. But, as always, Goethe held the place of honor.

When she was young she yearned for this love. Oma wasn't able to stay at her university in Germany—a university that had a plaque on its ancient stone walls stating *Goethe Was Here*. She had to go home and work—rather like Jo, due to wartime deprivation. Being female also had something to do with her lack, but eventually, in the United States, my step-grandfather 'allowed' her to finally pursue a higher education. At that point she developed an intellectual crush on her German professor, with whom she discussed literature, philosophy, and who knows what else. She did the same with me, excitedly telling me about her reading of Schopenhauer even as she was dying of cancer.

All of this comes to me as I read *Little Women* again and delve more into Louisa May Alcott herself. I nearly fall off my chair when I read in some of her autobiographical works just how much she loved Goethe—how she'd sing "Mignon's Song" under the window of Ralph Waldo Emerson, convinced that that romantic and intellectual older man was her "Master." My heart pounds a little when I come across a footnote in her published journals, referring to Goethe as her "chief idol."

I can only think of two things: I wish my Oma were here so I could share this exciting kinship, and reading these autobiographical writings vindicates my preference for Jo's choice of Professor Bhaer. I know that Laurie is the much-lamented would-be lover, but I just can't get behind it—in the book or on the screen. I didn't read the novel until I was a teenager, but even then he struck me as just an immature boy like all the immature boys I already knew. I also know that Louisa confessed to creating the professor out of pique, making, as she put it, "a funny match for Jo," because she was annoyed by her fans constantly asking her who the *Little Women* would marry. But was it such a funny match?

Jo is an unusual character, like Louisa herself, who does not necessarily want the life her marriageable sisters will have. She literally does not want the boy next door. With Louisa's intense interest in the German Romantics and Weimar Classicism—Goethe in particular—her creation of someone to fit an ideal of what she wanted for her own fictional alter-ego makes complete sense to me. Of course, in the novel, Professor Bhaer is a little too paternalistic and he criticizes Jo's stories (the very type of sensation story that Louisa herself preferred to write), which was changed in the Armstrong film to suit modern sensibilities. Indeed, Gabriel Byrne's soft-spoken professor lovingly pushes Jo to reach her full potential. Theirs is a more equal relationship than that of an older man teaching a younger woman.

Still. When Professor Bhaer arrives on the scene at Jo's boarding house whistling "Mignon's Song" from Goethe's masterpiece *Wilhelm Meister*, which Louisa sang under Emerson's window years before in the throes of intellectual passion, I know that Jo ends up with the right man. For Laurie does not touch her mind—her intellect and her imagination—which seems to be the key to opening her heart.

I inherited Oma's bust of Goethe when she died, as well as a love of books and a propensity to have crushes on German professors. I would love to tell her that Louisa May Alcott—and through her, Jo March—belonged to our club of Goethe-worshippers, and that they idealized men modeled after that German romantic sensibility inherent in him—just like we do, even if we don't end up with them. I'm sure my Oma would be just as excited and say how wonderful literature is because it is as real as life itself.

## About the Author

***K.R. Karr*** is a writer and academic who, like Jo March, falls into a "vortex" when putting pen to paper. She lives on the West Coast.

# Both Useful and Pleasant

*by Michelle J. Andrew*

❧

Do you know who Wallace and Gromit are? Maybe you've seen *The Nightmare Before Christmas* or *The Boxtrolls*? Well, that's me. No, not a Boxtroll exactly, but that's where I'd like to be—behind the scenes making one of those films.

I'm a stop-motion animator. I'm one of those rare, eccentric people who like to make very small puppets and furniture and little tiny pens and lamps and shoes, screw them to a table, move them the tiniest fraction and then take a picture. Then move them another tiny fraction and take another picture. Then repeat that several hundred times. That's what stop-motion animators do. For me, it's a magical experience to create something that's just like the real world but a whole lot smaller and then make it move, give it a life of its own. For me, Louisa did that too. She gave life to her characters in her writing.

In 2014 I was 41 years old and had spent 20 years writing statistical programs in an office. My days had been useful but quite a long way from pleasant. So I did the most obvious thing—I quit work to start an undergraduate degree in stop-motion animation and puppetry.

My classmates were all 20 years younger than me and collectively called me 'Mum'. We spent our days making stuff with plasticine, drawing flip books and seeing how real we could make fake grass. It was brilliant. I went on to start a self-designed master's degree in stop-motion and I'm two thirds through that (having had a baby at the end of my first year, as you do).

I like films that make you feel something, so I didn't want to make children's cartoons. I wanted to make something a little more poignant, something that you would come away from seeing with a tear in your eye or a little bit of your heart touched with an indelible memory. So my first film, *Colour Your Life*, was about an old lady called Enid who is sent one of her old 70s disco dresses by her granddaughter and decides that she isn't so old after all. Not too old for a bit of a dance, anyway.

I was going to make my own animated adaptation of *Little Women*. It was a classic I'd grown up with and I loved it to bits. Then I discovered that Louisa May Alcott had written many other books, and they were all just as wonderful—from fairytales to psychological thrillers—so I was spoilt for choice. When I delved into biographies of this amazingly determined, spirited and mirthful woman I found that her real life was even stranger than fiction and I was hooked. I consumed everything I could find about her. My tutor pointed out that it was the relationship between Louisa and Lulu, her niece, that was the most interesting part of my research. That relationship became the inspiration for *Windfall*, the stop-motion short film I'm now working on.

Louisa unexpectedly became a mother at age 46. Her younger sister May had married a young Swiss man called Ernest and they had moved to an idyllic apartment in Meudon, just outside of Paris. Sadly, May died a few weeks after childbirth and it was her dying wish that baby Lulu be sent to Concord, Massachusetts, for Louisa to raise as her own. This was both a blessing and a challenge for Louisa. She had little remaining strength for the noisy disruption a young child brings, but she loved her dearly and Lulu brought sunlight and purpose into her aunt's dull and tedious life, providing Louisa with the perfect reason why she had been 'spared' for greater things.[1]

Making my film has lead me to study the most intricate details of Louisa's life, her letters, her love for Lulu, her relationship with her family, how she dressed, how she wore her hair, where she lived, how she spoke even which variety of apples she ate, and the shining light and hope that Lulu brought into the family. In fact, I am not ashamed to say I have become entirely obsessed with this most wonderful woman and will talk endlessly about her to anyone who will listen.

Each of my days is now both useful and a good bit more than pleasant. My time is now fulfilling, satisfying, magical, enlightening and with more variety than exists in the apple kingdom, which is saying something. Indeed, the whole thing makes me incredibly happy (if quite tired with eye strain and rather rough hands). To

---

1 Alcott, L. M. (1890). *Louisa May Alcott: Her Life, Letters and Journals* (E. D. Cheney, ed.). Boston: Roberts Brothers, p. 316. Louisa compares her own life to May's idyll in Meudon, Paris: "*I dawdle about, and wait to see if I am to live or die. If I live, it is for some new work. I wonder what?*" From June / July: "[Louisa's health is] *improving fast, in spite of dark predictions and forebodings. The Lord has more work for me, so I am spared.*" See also p. 324: "*I see now why I lived,—to care for May's child and not leave Anna all alone.*"

misquote my dear Miss Alcott[1], my return to youth is delightful, my old age (and it's not far off now) will hold only a few regrets and yes … maybe there is a chance life will become a beautiful success.

I hope one day audiences—both staunch Louisa fans and those who are yet to make the pleasure of her acquaintance—will see my little masterpiece, learn to love this woman too, and go away with a small, determined, courageous, amusing yet rather cramped and ink-stained little handprint on their hearts too.

## About the author

***Michelle J. Andrew*** is a mature student studying for a master's degree in stop-motion animation at Staffordshire University, UK. She happily returned to university after spending 20 years in an office writing statistical programs. She now idles away her days nurturing her creative side and playing to her inner child by covering herself in paint, glue and sawdust while sticking, drawing, sculpting, sanding, designing and carving miniature props and sewing pretty little dresses for her animation puppets. She is a single parent of two lovely but spirited little souls, one of 2 years and one of 9. She relates intensely to Louisa becoming a mother at age 46.

1 Alcott, L.M. (2004). *Little Women.* New York: Signet Classic, last paragraph of Chapter 11: "*'I'll do my lessons every day, and not spend so much time with my music and dolls. I am a stupid thing, and ought to be studying, not playing,' was Beth's resolution, while Amy followed their example by heroically declaring, 'I shall learn to make buttonholes, and attend to my parts of speech.'*"

Michelle lives on the bottom edge of the Peak District in rural England, on the estate of a manor house surrounded by fields, sheep and one particularly enchanting owl with her two boys, a grey-whiskered border collie and a cat called Lulu.

She hopes that Louisa would approve of being immortalizing in the shape of a six-inch puppet but she suspects Louisa would tell her to go and do something more useful instead.

# I *Lime* Amy March

*by Merry Gordon*

ᔓ

Of all the literary indignities committed upon me in my youth, Amy March was top of the heap. From the "injured sniff" of her first line to the last glimpse of her as madonna à la mode, that self-important, social climbing little snot got under my skin.

I hated her for her blonde curls and blue eyes. I hated her DIY clothespin nose job. I hated her stupid lime fiasco. I hated the way her efforts at being "good" amounted to a snit about the inconvenience of waiting until Aunt March kicked off before she snagged the old bat's turquoise ring. Most of all, I hated her because (with some exceptions) the girl just kept winning: the steady stream of male attention, the Europe trip, the rich, young and handsome husband. If *Little Women* is a game show, Beth's out by the second round, Meg and Jo get lovely parting gifts in the form of twins and bookish Germans, but Amy? Cue the balloons and confetti drop: Amy March is your grand prize winner.

Years ago, when pressed by a friend about my hatred for Amy, my argument went something like this: "She's just so *fake*. She fakes everything to make herself look better. She only wins because she gets good enough at faking that nobody questions it anymore."

This earned me a side-eye from my friend. "Yeah? I'd like to meet the woman who isn't doing that same thing."

Her reaction gave me pause. Twelve-year-old Amy is indeed a *poseur*. Still, every affectation, every obnoxious fad—all of it was calculated to bring her the measure of social and economic success she craved.

I'd been there too. I'd had, like Amy, "ever so many wishes" … wishes that (like hers) thankfully matured over time. But my beginnings were just as awkward and ill-advised.

A picture of me in middle school circa 1990 proclaims this truth. At least Amy had the sense to leave her hair alone. In my adolescent glory, I had teased my bangs a full four inches above my head. I trailed a cloud of hairspray so vast it might have warranted its own Al Gore documentary. The popular girls managed a sort of sexily tangled waterfall effect like the backup singers in a Mötley Crüe music video, but my hair looked more like a wad of raffia perched upon a Styrofoam ball, the sort of 3rd grade craft project that gets a pity B from the teacher.

I committed fashion crimes against humanity to fit in, things so ludicrous you could forgive Amy her accessorizing with shrubbery when she meets Laurie in Nice. I wore leggings in abstract fluorescent patterns, a sort of Picasso-meets-*Saved-By-The-Bell* vibe. Heaven help me, they were stirrup leggings. Like every tween fashionista of the early 90s, I had more stirrups in my closet than a stable full of gynecologists.

And the shoes … all the pretty girls wore Keds, those flimsy, overpriced, white canvas sneakers that probably cost about $.99 to make in some Indonesian sweatshop.

(The $29 you paid on top of that was for the iconic blue rubber tag that announced you a member of the in crowd, of course.) We couldn't afford real Keds, but desperate times called for desperate measures: I took a blue Sharpie to the back of my knock-offs and hoped nobody would notice from afar. Remember when Jo outs Amy for painting her white boots blue? #Relatable.

I crimped. I pegged. I scrunched. I faked. Was a happily ever after with Kelly Kapowski's hair and Paula Abdul's dance moves too much to ask? There weren't enough mix tapes or Ring Pops in the world to console me over my juvenile gawkiness.

It wasn't until far into my post-Aqua Net apocalypse years that I realized the actual effort inherent in the long con that is maturation. I had young Amy all wrong. What I had been unable to recognize was that "lapses of lingy" and lobster luncheon fails notwithstanding, Amy March isn't faking as much as she's *working it.*

Alcott is clear about her ambition in Chapter Ten, when Amy takes on the persona of Dickens' Nathaniel Winkle: Amy "was always trying to do what she couldn't."

Except eventually, she succeeded.[2]

Sure, she was imperfect, and occasionally vain, and certainly misguided a time or two (remember the plaster foot molding incident?), but that girl just put herself out there time and time again. She got it wrong more than she got it right, but she kept trying.

And not only is Amy March working it, she's growing. Out of all Alcott's girls, she's the one with the

2 Well, sort of. I mean, ideally, girlfriend would've hacked her way to the top in the art world *and* snagged the guy, but in 19th century America women didn't usually get to have their cake and eat it too.

most dynamic character arc. Fortunately for me and for Amy, hard-won spiritual development doesn't require a substantial hair product budget or satin slippers. I nixed the mall bangs for a mom 'do and a shot at the in crowd for a shot at inspiration. By the end of *Good Wives*, Amy upgrades her calling cards and gold digger daydreams for the "better wealth of love, confidence, and happiness."

The thing is, love, confidence and happiness don't just tumble from the sky into your lap. They demand pursuit. They demand ambition. And ambition demands failure, revision, and what we sometimes call 'faking' it as we grow, and learn, and prioritize, and *re*-prioritize our lives. We change. We try and fail and try again. We keep up appearances.

There's something of a posh veneer over the life of Laurie's leading lady by the time Alcott's tale draws to a close. As I reevaluate the happy familial tableau at the end of the book, I can't help but wonder: does Amy sweat under that mountain of silk? Perhaps her postpartum corset digs into her ribs a little more than it used to. What's the lovely Mrs. Laurence covering up?

Alcott demurs on such subjects and leaves Amy on her pedestal. But I know her better than that now.

I recently gave a speech to a large group. Just ten minutes before, I had used my earring post to perform what amounted to minor dental surgery in trying to extract a piece of granola bar wedged between my teeth. A furious Netflix binge the night before meant that I'd skipped washing my hair (again) and was now praying to the dry shampoo gods to hold 3-day-old waves in place. My white-knuckled death grip on the podium disguised trembling hands.

What the audience saw was a woman outwardly at ease with a microphone, clicking around in killer four-inch fire engine red power heels. Hair? Perfect. Lips? Glossy. Stance? Confident. I looked passionate and intentional.

"How do you do it?" another friend asked after I spoke. "I *hate* you," she said, in that half-joking, half-serious way women have.

Inwardly, I laughed. What I knew—what I suspect all Amy Marches know—is that behind every seemingly self-assured, fulfilled woman is a trail of "commy la fo" and bad plaster casts and purple dresses with yellow polka-dots and stringy chicken salad.

"Ambitious girls have a hard time," says Amy to Laurie at one point. She's right, but not in the way she means it. Amy's talking about civil and material aid that could boost the chances of a struggling middle-class girl like she once was. But ambitious women today have a hard time in a way that goes beyond money and class. We prize perfection. We stigmatize failure. We compete—but against each other's filtered, faux Insta-realities, instead of against our own best. In a before/after world, we tend to cover up our growth instead of embracing it, and then we call each other out for 'faking' it.

I have come to see Amy as a sister, a kindred spirit. Somewhere underneath "her ladyship" is a little girl who obsessed over pickled limes and dreamed of a Grecian nose, just like somewhere under my pin-up pumps and poise is the tween who colored in the backs of her fake Keds and scripted phone-in pizza orders because talking to strangers was too awkward. I have come to love all those versions of Amy—and all those versions of me. They prove that we are capable of evolution.

Amy is the most human of the March sisters, even more so than Jo. She is flawed—not in a sympathetic way, like her wild older sister, but in a way that holds the mirror up to ourselves, a way that can get uncomfortable. Amy starts out conceited. Petty. Superficial. She is a name-dropper and a status-seeker. She's inept and fumbling in her attempts at grace. Somehow, she manages to grow past that and into a woman worthy of our respect and admiration, ruling over Parnassus, if Louisa May Alcott is to be believed, with "gentle dignity."

Which gives me hope that someday, I might be able to do the same.

Dammit, Amy March. I guess I kinda love you after all.

## About the Author

***Merry Gordon*** is a reader, a writer, an editor, and a teacher. She will, in true Jo March fashion, fire pillows at you should you dare to disrupt her when "genius burns"—unless it's to bring her chocolate or more books.

# Finding the Palace Beautiful

*by KL Allendoerfer*

ᔓᔕ

I recently finished reading a book about introversion called *Quiet: The Power of Introverts in a World that Can't Stop Talking*, by Susan Cain. At the same time I was in the middle of re-reading *Little Women* to my 7th grade daughter, and my daughter asked me who my favorite character was. Hers was Jo, of course. A church friend of mine loves Jo too, and has written academic papers on her. And even another friend who was named Amy after Amy March still cites Jo as her favorite. Going with the flow, I pointed out to my daughter that there was indeed something pretty cool about moving to New York and meeting and marrying a German man (which is what I did myself 15 years ago). These days I think it's almost impossible to be a bookish girl of a certain age (or almost any age) and not admire Jo. Modeled on her creator, Louisa May Alcott, Jo became a wildly successful author in a time when most women did not have careers outside the home.

Upon re-reading a book that I last read more than 30 years ago, however, I'm stumbling upon some uncomfortable truths. I remember now that it took me a few tries to get through *Little Women* at all when I was a kid. The tone struck me as a little too preachy, and everybody—even the supposedly flawed and temperamental Jo—was a little too sweet and perfect.

What's most remarkable to me, though, is that while, as an adult, I admire Jo and consider her an interesting and appropriate role model for my own spirited daughter, I'm remembering now that when I first read the book, my favorite character, the one I identified with the most, was not Jo at all. It was Beth: quiet, introverted Beth—even then, an outlier in a world that couldn't stop talking. Jo, by contrast, was a little scary, and the opposite of me: she was jolly, and extroverted, and talked to boys easily.

Many days I envied Beth that she was allowed to be homeschooled. I liked that she petted and favored and was comforted by a beat-up old doll. More than anything, though, what I liked about Beth was that she was a musician, a pianist whose playing brought pleasure to family and friends at home. Beth's musicianship didn't extend to concertizing or giving recitals, however, and she played the fancy grand piano of Mr. Laurence, her wealthy next-door neighbor, only when she thought no one else was listening.

There has been some scholarship on Beth. One commentator points out that Beth is a version of a $19^{th}$ century stock character, the "Angel in the House," a character that Virginia Woolf wrote had to be killed in order for women artists to assert their creative independence. Louisa, by having Beth die in the second half of *Little Women*, appears to have largely agreed with this assessment, perhaps foreshadowing Woolf. I never quite forgave Louisa for killing off Beth, even though the book was semi-autobiographical. In fiction, why not let her grow up and become a beloved piano teacher, lavishing all the love and care on her students that she lavished on her dolls? I took Beth's death a little personally.

The commentators are right in one way, at least: society doesn't seem to know what to do with introverts. It's certainly viewed as a tidier and more dramatic story if the quiet ones are pushed off the literary stage one way or another, leaving the real, interesting business of literature to those who heroically take risks and self-actualize. From reading *Quiet*, it appears not much has changed, in literature or anywhere else. If anything, the pro-extrovert bias has gotten stronger in the 20$^{th}$ and 21$^{st}$ centuries. In situations from school, to work, to church, people are exhorted to "put themselves out there" and work collaboratively in large groups. Introverts are called antisocial, shamed, and weeded out in job interviews by misapplied Myers-Briggs tests.

Reading *Quiet*, I, like many others, felt a shock of recognition. I felt like I could almost have written the book myself. In particular, it described virtually my entire early career playing the violin: dislike of performing, not wanting people to hear me play—a desire, like Beth, to play music alone or only for people I knew rather than strangers. And it describes the subsequent shame and feeling of being defective since I didn't fit society's "Extrovert Ideal—the omnipresent belief that the ideal self is gregarious, alpha and comfortable in the spotlight."[1]

But I didn't write the book myself, and in my relief at having my basic introversion validated in print, at first I missed an important part of Cain's thesis: that introverts and extroverts both complement and need each other.

---

1 Cain, S. (2013). *Quiet: The Power of Introverts in a World that Can't Stop Talking.* New York: Broadway Books, p. 4.

What's out of balance in modern times is that the extrovert ideal is taking up too much space. Rather than merely saying defensively that introverts are too just as good as extroverts, Cain makes the case that introversion, with its allowance for and consideration of fear, uncertainty, and doubt, provides a much-needed check on overreaching. She points out that throughout history there has always been an important creative tension between thought and action, between the philosopher and the king. She highlights the working relationship between introverted Rosa Parks and extroverted Martin Luther King Jr. as a particularly meaningful partnership in the civil rights movement. Introverts, with their tendency to look before they leap, are more likely to be able to see and avert impending disasters. In fact, Jo March knew this too: she needed Beth's quiet counsel as a check on her own impulses. Jo describes Beth as "her conscience" and has a special, close relationship with her of mutual respect.

A particularly important and damaging myth that Cain takes on in *Quiet* is the perception that introverts are antisocial or don't care about others. She provides many examples of introverts rising to the occasion and creating something meaningful in a relationship. And she also makes the case that introverted artists, with their self-awareness and sensitivity, can make great performers if they choose to, and if their gifts aren't squelched by damaging labels applied to their personalities.

In *Little Women*, at the end of the chapter "Beth Finds the Palace Beautiful," Jo suggests as a joke that Beth go over and thank Mr. Laurence for his kindnesses. To everyone's surprise and delight, Beth rises to the occasion:

> She went and knocked at the study door before she gave herself time to think, and when a gruff voice called out, come in! she did go in, right up to Mr. Laurence, who looked quite taken aback, and held out her hand, saying, with only a small quaver in her voice, "I came to thank you, sir, for—" but she didn't finish, for he looked so friendly that she forgot her speech and, only remembering that he had lost the little girl he loved, she put both arms round his neck and kissed him .... Beth ceased to fear him from that moment, and sat there talking to him as cozily as if she had known him all her life, for love casts out fear, and gratitude can conquer pride.

Even in the re-reading, I temporarily stalled on the "Valley of the Shadow" chapter. I hope that now, in the 21st century, Beth no longer has to die for Jo to succeed. Both Beth and Jo deserve better.

## ABOUT THE AUTHOR

***KL Allendoerfer*** is a science educator, musician, and writer. She spent her early career working in biotech and raising her children in the Boston area, where she learned to play the violin again after many years off. She loved *Little Women* growing up, but mostly forgot about it until she started reading her childhood copy of the book to her school-age daughter. She and her daughter then re-discovered Orchard House on a coming-of-age tour with their Unitarian-Universalist church. She now lives with her German computer scientist husband and their teenage children in Silicon Valley, California. She blogs regularly at *A Thousand Finds* and occasionally at *Violinist.com* and is currently at work on a near-future science fiction series set in the New England region of a newly federalized North America.

# Piccole Donne

*by Lorraine Tosiello*

ଓ

The table is so big that it nearly takes up the entire space in the kitchen. One door off the kitchen leads to the lone bedroom, the other to the living room that doubles as the girls' sleeping room. The girls sit around the gleaming white enamel surface with their mother, her two sisters and their girl cousins. The five girls grow up together like sisters, even sharing an unusual entryway between their two apartments, a door from the foyer to the next door living room, which allows them to skirt back and forth between the two households without going into the public hallway of the New York City tenement.

Today they are working in unison, bent over the green tape, aluminum wire and silk petals, which they twirl and paste expertly into artificial flowers. They love to make the flowers together, the methodical, soothing, rapid movements of their fingers smoothing the tension of the day into visible beauty. They talk, they sigh, they plan, as they produce a pile of pink peonies, white camellias and red rose buds.

Another day they might be making ravioli, which they spread out on the bed on clean white sheets to dry, or delicious, soft anisette cookies, twisted into knots and frosted with white glaze. But always, they work together, no men interrupting the female industry. This household is the domain of women.

The mothers are careful to speak only English, not lapsing into Italian phrases. Their daughters will be little American women. They decide they will need local help to make their daughters rise above the superstitions and restrictions of their native background. The immigrant women apply to the local church, the Judson, seeking advice on raising their daughters the American way. The nurses and social workers there give advice on nutrition and education. They visit the homes and see the clean sheets, the hearty food, the bonds of family and know that their services are not really needed. The only thing these women need is the confidence to face the changes ahead as they emerge from the domestic circle into the modern world. The social worker leaves a book that will appeal to the sorority the women embrace, while showing them all the potential a confident woman can achieve. The book looks like a simple children's tale. It is called *Little Women.*

ఌ

Christmas in an Italian household is always the most magnificent day of the year. My sister and I had dresses with scratchy crinoline underskirts and velvet waist bands. Our patent leather shoes squeezed too tightly in the heat of my grandmother's apartment. The door between the two apartments was open and people circulated back and forth. The ravioli were boiling in pots on both stoves and the steam increased the heat and fogged the men's glasses.

There was only room for a tiny artificial tree perched atop the coffee table. But the good cheer and the feasting and the presents were endless. My sister and I had a special present to share from our aunts. It was a real adult book, with lots of words and hundreds of pages. Inside a stiff grey slipcase, the book had illustrations of girls in dresses more confining than our own. The girls were singing together around a piano, or traipsing together through the snow, or sitting around a chair while their mother reads a letter. *Little Women*.

That September, we moved to the suburbs. There were no statues or crucifixes in the airy modern classroom. The teacher had a smart pencil skirt and a sweater set that rivaled Jackie Kennedy's, instead of the wimple and habit of the nuns at my previous school. The principal was pleased to state that I was an intelligent girl. "She read *Little Women* in the first grade," she whispered to the teacher. The teacher smiled and showed me the classroom corner with more age appropriate books. But I knew better.

The following year, *Little Women* was the first novel I read, but I did not stop there. I was determined to read every book in the children's library. I started with the As and thought that if I read three books a week I would get through it all before graduation. When I got to the middle of the C authors, I reached a series of books for boys. They were grey books with red lettering in the spine, glamorized fictions about boys in different capacities in American wars. There were about a half dozen of the offending books. I could not bear the thought of wading through all of them. It made no sense to say I would read every book in the library except the grey books about boys in wars, so I stopped my challenge. I once returned to that peaceful neighborhood library and the grey books were no longer there. Of course, the A shelf remained full of Alcott novels, and the stories of the girl heroes I had absorbed into my very self: Jo March, Polly Milton, Rose Campbell and Nan Harding.

By the mid-1960s, the four little women were thrown over for four little men from England. As the March family had piloted me safely through grade school, the Beatles would be my guideposts through middle school. Now every American girl claimed her status by choosing her Beatle instead of her March sister. Of course, I was a John girl. A John girl would tolerate no shams, communicate in sarcasm and strive relentlessly to change the world. Or was that a Jo March girl? The year of the woman in 1968 followed soon after. Jo March was swallowed up in the progress of Betty Friedan and Gloria Steinem.

Being the intelligent girl that the principal had encouraged, I went on to medical school (thank you, Nan!), never overtly aware of how Alcott's heroines led me forward. For years the only reading I would do was medical texts and journals. To read anything else would be a disservice to my patients. The journals piled up next to my bedside and I slogged through them diligently. My daughters did not read *Little Women* and I did not see the need to direct them there, for they had Harry Potter, Mulan and Beyoncé.

❧

Five years ago, having raised my family and accomplished enough in my academic medicine career, my children were grown, my professional and academic goals were complete. Even the desperate urgency of my field in HIV medicine had calmed to a manageable office-based practice. I decided to work part time. I still had five aunts who had lived well into their eighties. I would spend my first free afternoons days visiting them, and my first free nights reading. I was reading fiction for the first time since leaving college. I read Dostoevsky and Hurston, Saramago and Perec, Flaubert and Calvino. I read and read and made lists of books still to read.

Among my disjointed reading, I had reluctantly re-read a popular book from the year of my medical internship, called *The House of God*. I had been flooded with suppressed memories of the harrowing and difficult conditions medical trainees experienced in the 1980s. I was shaken by refinding my younger self in a more real way than I even remembered. The same thing happened with *Little Women*. Suddenly, I saw the girl I was trying to become in all of Jo March's trials. I looked at my girl cousins, every one a teacher, or caregiver, or health professional. Every one encouraged by the deep-seated lessons of the March family. I returned instinctively to the hopes and dreams of a generation of American immigrant women, our grandmothers, who, around a gleaming white table, would learn the power their domestic actions had to change society, the redeeming quality of diligent work, and the embracing comfort and support of a circle of strong women. As true American girls of the mid-20th century, my family seemed to embody Louisa May Alcott's vision of the power and promise of women in society. I recalled my rebellious teenage self, who knew that every profession was possible for a woman. I remembered the deep-seated lessons of the March family:

to work diligently for the right, never shirk daily duties, and always to relying on your sisters for sustenance.

All the women in my family, it seems, were in essence Little Women.

## About the Author

***Lorraine Tosiello*** first read *Little Women* at age six and missed most of the pathos and substance, but could not miss the boisterous, large, forceful personality of Jo March. She wanted to be able to charge off to sweep the snow, talk to boys and make a mess of things just as she did. That pretty much never changed.

She is a physician and has dedicated her entire life to the care of people with HIV infection. She has published some medical articles and a monograph, *A History of the Medical Profession in Westfield, New Jersey.*

Since starting to work part time several years ago, she has been immersed in the work and times of Louisa May Alcott and is currently working on two historical fiction books about her.

Pink Umbrella Books is a Phoenix-based indie micropublisher committed to connecting readers with quality books.

A full-service publisher, Pink Umbrella Books also offers à la carte services for indie authors, including:

Professional editing
Custom book covers
Book layout and design
eBook formatting
Book trailers
Author website design and setup

Email us at info@pinkumbrellabooks.com

pinkumbrellapublishing.com